A Winter comedy follows the Spring of *The Lady's not for Burning* and the Autumn of *Venus Observed*. The play revolves around a dramatic incident in the Hungarian revolution against the Austro-Hungarian Empire in 1848-9. The Austrian countess emerges as one of Fry's most striking personalities; the other characters are sharp but tuned to be her subordinates—her contradictory daughter Gelda, her weak son Stefan, the wastrel Gettner, and the well-meaning Count Peter. Here is Fry at his best, combining comic and serious episodes with a clear sense of situation and intent.

The story is almost outside the strict limits of comedy, but as Fry himself says: 'There is an angle of experience where the dark is distilled into light: either here or hereafter, in or out of time: where our tragic fate finds itself with perfect pitch, and goes straight to the key which creation was composed in. And comedy serves and reaches out to this experience. It says, in effect, that, groaning as we may be, we move in the figure of a dance, and so moving, we trace the outline of the mystery.'

is now famous in both British and American theater. He has directed, produced, and written all kinds of theater productions—from musicals to verse plays to pageants. It is in more recent years that his main series of plays. *The Firstborn, A P...... The .... begins with Ang...... ....ound the .... The Lady ....b of Priso...... .....been ....

THE DARK IS
LIGHT ENOUGH

CHRISTOPHER FRY

THE DARK IS
LIGHT ENOUGH

A Winter Comedy

OXFORD UNIVERSITY PRESS

NEW YORK AND LONDON

To

LENA ASHWELL

with affection and admiration

CHRISTOPHER FRY   EDITH EVANS

CHARACTERS

IN ORDER OF APPEARANCE

JAKOB

KASSEL

BELMANN

STEFAN

BELLA

WILLI

GELDA

RICHARD GETTNER

COUNTESS ROSMARIN OSTENBURG

COLONEL JANIK

COUNT PETER ZICHY

1ST SOLDIER

2ND SOLDIER

3RD SOLDIER

1ST GUARD

2ND GUARD

*An Austrian country-house
near the Hungarian border*

The winter of 1848–9

*The weather was stormy; the sky heavily clouded;
the darkness . . . profound. . . . It was across
this maze of leafage, and in absolute darkness,
that the butterflies had to find their way in
order to attain the end of their pilgrimage.*

*Under such conditions the screech-owl would
not dare to forsake its olive-tree. The butterfly . . .
goes forward without hesitation. . . . So well it
directs its tortuous flight that, in spite of all
the obstacles to be evaded, it arrives in a state
of perfect freshness, its great wings intact. . . .
The darkness is light enough. . . .*

J. H. FABRE

THE DARK IS
LIGHT ENOUGH

ACT ONE

A room and a great staircase

JAKOB. KASSEL.

Enter BELMANN.

JAKOB. Tell us, then, what in the world has happened?
Are we never to have any more Thursdays, Belmann?

BELMANN. The Countess is nowhere in the house.

KASSEL.   I guessed as much
Before I was over the threshold..In fact
I had the thought of it half a mile away.
'I suppose this *is* Thursday', I said to myself,
And looked at my watch.

BELMANN.   She drove away, alone,
Before light this morning.

JAKOB.   Alone?

BELMANN.   All the servants
Swear by heaven it's impossible, and by God
There's no doubt of it. One of them woke,
Or dreamt he woke, and heard, or thought he heard,
The great sleigh making for the Thiereck gate.
But now the snow's so deep there's no way of telling.

JAKOB. Not even towards Vienna? Towards Thiereck?
I wonder if she knows where the Hungarian troops are.
Surely she must have heard they're advancing?

[1]

KASSEL.   With
    A son-in-law in the War Ministry, she may well believe
    They're where they were two months ago, still
    Fighting the Serbs.

JAKOB.   Do you think this is the time
    To joke, Dr. Kassel? Think of the Countess.

KASSEL. I do, and the snow immediately melts
    And all the Hungarians are dead.

JAKOB. But she left in absolute secret, before light,
    Quite alone, and in this weather—

KASSEL.   And on a Thursday,
    That's the worst of it.

JAKOB.   What are you mocking, Kassel?

KASSEL. I? Mocking? Dear fellow, my dear boy,
    Nothing that doesn't mock me in return.

JAKOB. Isn't it true that in more than twenty years
    She has only once before failed her Thursday,
    When her son Stefan was born?

KASSEL.   Not even once.
    'Good God', she said, 'I think the monkey
    Means to be born on Thursday evening.'
    But she received us all at seven o'clock,
    And at nine, when Gyorki was saying, as usual,
    That there is no clear truth except the present
    Which alters as we grasp it,
    She bowed to us in the doorway, and said
    'We must freely admit the future', and withdrew
    To give birth to Stefan.

JAKOB.   But what future
    Can make her withdraw today and abandon her Thursday?

[2]

A message of two lines would have put our minds
At rest.

KASSEL.   Do you think so? I have always found
Her handwriting to be her way, not
Of giving but of withholding information.
Don't we hear her now?

Enter STEFAN.

KASSEL. Well, Stefan, where's your mother?

STEFAN.   That's just it,
Doctor Kassel, where's my mother?
The whole day I've been riding the country-side
Asking every person I could find.
One said he caught the sound of bells in the dark,
But the rest had never heard of a human being
Since they last went to mass. But she may tell you
Herself. Here's a letter for you.

KASSEL.   Where did you find this?

STEFAN. Face-downwards. I've only this moment discovered it.

BELMANN. Now, Kassel. What has she to say? What is the answer
To the mystery?

KASSEL.   She has taken some pains with this.
One guesses almost at once that words are meant.
Ah, yes. You see, now. In this world a mystery
Is only so out of extreme simplicity.

JAKOB. Read it, Kassel.

KASSEL.   Yes, of course. She says:
'Dear my little doctor, if, and I don't
Know why it should be, when the evening comes
I am still not with you, do make my excuses.
Tell them not to talk about—', but here

[3]

The marks on the paper leave one a wide margin
Of possibility. Three words, apparently
Entirely composed of E's. 'Tell them not
To talk about Ee*lee*leeology,
Ee*lee*leeology, OR Ee*lee*leeology.
The world is more serious than that.
I have gone out. Your affectionate
Rosmarin Ostenburg.'

JAKOB.   But I don't see, Kassel,
What we're supposed to make of it.

BELMANN.   As Kassel says,
It's only too simple. The Countess, impatient
Of the doctor's attention, has gone out:
To pay a call, or to take a breath of air,
But for rather more than twelve hours, and in
The direction of a war.

STEFAN.   But will you tell me
What I should have done, or do now, if my mother's lost?

BELMANN. Ah, there we have the difficulty.
This Thursday world of ours is now
More like the world than ever.
The goddess of it, in her Godlike way,
Is God knows where. We can only hope
She will condescend to appear in her own time.

JAKOB. No, no; we must be anxious. I should have
No peace for a moment if I thought I lacked anxiety.
You might pray for her safety, Belmann,
Instead of inventing crackpot blasphemies.

BELMANN. Blasphemies? Why do you think I blaspheme?
You know the Countess has the qualities of true divinity.
For instance: how apparently undemandingly

[4]

She moves among us; and yet
Lives make and unmake themselves in her neighbourhood
As nowhere else. There are many names I could name
Who would have been remarkably otherwise
Except for her divine non-interference.

KASSEL. Good heavens, she would rather be dead
Than be responsible for any change
In any soul in the world.

BELMANN.   She can't escape it.
If she should die, her gravestone would play havoc
With the life of the mason who carved it.
She has a touching way
Of backing a man up against eternity
Until he hardly has the nerve to remain mortal.

STEFAN. My first thought, as it always is,
Was to tell my brother-in-law the trouble.
To me Peter treads the earth more surely
And reassures more instantly
Than any other man. So instinctively
In the morning panic, I sent a message
To Peter and my sister in Vienna.

KASSEL. Have you had an answer?

STEFAN.   Nothing yet.
But Peter's the great protector of the family.
If you call to him, he puts his own world down
And takes yours up, almost before you realize
What made you need him.
But I thought none of you would be here tonight.
We're in the direct road of the revolution.
The peasants are saying their dogs haven't stopped barking
Since before sunset. They hear the shake

[5]

Of marching in the earth. It's a wretched business.
The Hungarians have managed to exist
Happily enough in the Empire up to now.
And Peter is Hungarian, after all,
And still finds it possible to serve
In the Austrian Government.
But these Hungarian nationalists think they stand
For truth and light, and kill accordingly.
It would have been wiser to have stayed in Vienna.

BELMANN. My commitment, on Thursday evenings, is to be here.
After that I will be wise or not as I may be.
A man has to provide his own providence
Or there's no knowing what religion will get hold of him.

STEFAN. Why aren't you drinking? Make Bella bring you something.   [*He goes upstairs.*

KASSEL. Yes, yes; we won't let ourselves be forgotten.

BELMANN. All the servants are in their accustomed places;
Only the virtue has gone out of them.

[*He pulls a bell-rope.*

What, Kassel, you say the Countess would never
Change a soul? And yet you and I can remember
How ten years ago this great and good
Lady of our imagination
Conscripted her little daughter, Gelda,
Then aged—what was she, Kassel?—sixteen at most—

KASSEL. Seventeen.

BELMANN.   —then aged seventeen,
Into a marriage with that rag of hell
Richard Gettner: that invertebrate,
That self-drunk, drunken, shiftless, heartless,
Lying malingerer, Richard Gettner,

[6]

Than whom of all the tribe of men
There was no man more likely to make her wretched.

JAKOB. Liar, Belmann, a wicked lie!

BELMANN.   Did you ever
Know Richard Gettner?

JAKOB.   No, at school I read
His first book, whatever the name of it was,
When everyone said it would give literature
A new fire. I never met him,
Or read another.

BELMANN.   There wasn't another.
He fled from his one book as though his own
Reality had struck him on the mouth.
And then, on the profits from it, became a pest
Who never left us, and never loved us;
Unreliable when he was drunk,
Irresponsible when he was sober,
Useless to any world, sober or drunk.
But the Countess thought she should marry her daughter to him,
I imagine to celebrate the tenth reprinting.

JAKOB. The Countess can be sure, wherever she may be,
Her name is safe in this house, even though
It means the end of one of us, either you or me.
Discuss this with pistols, as soon as you like:
Tomorrow or Saturday.

BELMANN.   Don't be troublesome,
Jakob.

KASSEL. Preposterous. Ring the bell again.

JAKOB. No, no, I mean it. At last I can show myself
What these evenings have meant to me. I shall fight you.

[7]

BELMANN. We shall miss you, Jakob.
Let us, by all means, shoot at one another
If you think it will improve human nature.
And what is to happen after that?

JAKOB.   I'm only
Concerned with this moment of loyalty.

BELMANN.   I respect it:
But don't question my integrity.

JAKOB. Very well; I call you a liar.

BELMANN.   Well, so I sometimes am.
But don't question my integrity.
It was an act of dark night
To marry her daughter to him. And, thank God,
He was mad, or no man, or had some faint
Kick of conscience, enough to make him have mercy
And never touch her. And so for a time
She walked in his house looking in the mirrors
And after a few months came away,
And the Church dissolved all, as though
Mortal mistakes were snow; and she was married
To Count Peter the sturdy. By so small
A margin was misery missed and her mother undamned.

Enter BELLA, *and* WILLI, *a servant, with refreshment.*

KASSEL. Bella, we need you. We're thirsty, anxious,
And unattended. Why wouldn't you come to us?

BELLA. Dr. Kassel, you mustn't say so. If I could always do what's
impossible I should have very great advantages. But when you
rang the bell, she was there, with every bell on the harness
ringing, arriving at the old entrance.

KASSEL. Who arriving, Bella?

JAKOB. Do you mean the Countess? Is she home again, Bella?

BELLA. Then where is Willi, or Spier, you may say, or old Tenky? But don't think, because she can take herself off in the morning without help from a soul, she doesn't come back in the evening, looking as helpless as though no coat would come off without two able-bodied men to each sleeve.

BELMANN. In fact, the Countess is with us again.

KASSEL. Well, Bella, where has she been?

BELLA. She says she isn't at all certain because everywhere is so alike in the snow. She says she prayed to be punctual, but, considering the time of year, she didn't pray nearly enough. I'm just going up to her.

KASSEL. Tell her, if she's tired—and how the devil can she not be?—not to dream of coming down to us. It's a great foolishness. Tell her, if you like, I forbid it.

BELLA. You know very well, Dr. Kassel, she would come down before she was ready, in case you thought there was any doubt of it.

BELMANN. So after all, Willi, your mistress has come back, and it seems there's no trouble.

WILLI. That's it, sir. The gentleman has the trouble, dear God he has, I should say so, speaking in regard to him, sir.

BELMANN. Gentleman, Willi? What gentleman?

BELLA. Don't encourage him, sir. He sees gentlemen everywhere. Every day I have to tell him there's no such thing. Is there such a thing, Willi? Now think with your head.

WILLI. No, mam.

BELLA. So go downstairs, Willi.

WILLI. Yes, mam.

[*He goes.*

[9]

BELLA. It's best to say nothing, and the gentlemen pass off. We're none of us perfect. There's her bell again.

[*She goes away up the stairs.*

BELMANN. So saying, the world was emptied of men.

JAKOB. It would be all the better for it, if many men
Were as unmannered as you are.
To insinuate so, in front of a servant:
'What gentleman, Willi?' Are you trying deliberately
To infuriate me?

BELMANN.   Truth, Jakob,
Truth, is what my knees bow to.
Kassel, something approximating
To a suspicion of the truth has just occurred to me.
What more likely than that Richard Gettner's
Behind this mystery?

KASSEL.   Gettner?

BELMANN. Where is the onetime bridegroom now?

JAKOB. With the Hungarian army, I know, I heard that.

BELMANN. With the Hungarian army: off he went
Roaring into their arms, the great lover
Of his country's enemies. Indeed, loving
The enemy is almost the only commandment
He's never broken. Whoever hates his race,
His Emperor, his culture, or his mother
Wins—well, not his heart, which is apparently
Only locomotor,
But all the enthusiasm of his spleen.

BELLA *comes down the stairs with* STEFAN.

BELLA. Oh, goodness now, somebody's come, and I think it's

[10]

your sister, but what in the world, what a thing to do, if it is
your sister, what a thing to have happened in the circumstances.

STEFAN. Yes, Bella, what a thing to have happened. Is Count Peter
with her?

BELLA. How can I tell? The window's caked with snow, and you
breathe whatever you do. Well, I'll have a little word with her
first and give her fair warning, and that's the best I can do,
and there we are.

[*She hurries out.*

STEFAN [*to* KASSEL]. What mystery is there now?

KASSEL. Mystery, my dear boy? Because Bella is mysterious?
What nonsense.

A MAN *is slowly descending the stairs.*

BELMANN. No, but a little mystery there may be.
Willi has seen visions of gentlemen
Or at least one gentleman, to our perfect knowledge—

JAKOB. Belmann, I wish I could strike you dead!

BELMANN. On Saturday, Jakob. Don't fuss.

STEFAN.   Why, what goes on?
What gentleman?

Enter GELDA, *followed by* BELLA.

GELDA.   Stefan, what happened? Where
Did mother go?

BELLA.   If only you weren't so impatient
And had let me speak to you.

STEFAN.   Oh, Gelda, I'm sorry:
This was my bad blunder. Has Peter come?

[GELDA *is looking at the* MAN, *who has reached the foot of
the stairs.*

[11]

KASSEL [*turning*]. Richard Gettner!

BELLA. There it is, you see.
[*She goes out.*

JAKOB. Gettner?

BELMANN. Gettner, by God!

GETTNER. By God, no other.
I remember you, too, but without astonishment.
It's Thursday night. The intellectual soul
Of Europe comes down to the stream to drink. What's this
Floating belly-upwards? A dead fish?
Gettner, by God!

KASSEL. Now, come: why not allow us
A perfectly natural surprise?

BELMANN. We thought
You played games in a different alley now.

GETTNER. I'm surprised that you should have me in your thoughts.

GELDA. Richard, make me some sign of recognition.

GETTNER. Why? You must know I recognize you.
But then you also know, I suppose, the ten
Years have improved you to a kind of beauty,
And you'd like to see that I see that.
Well, if it gives you pleasure to be commended
By what remains of a bad husband,
Be pleased: I've noticed and admired.
Where's your *good* husband this vile night?

BELMANN. That's charming, Gettner.

GELDA. Peter will be here presently.
He said he would follow after, the first moment
He could manage to get away. We were both
Anxious for my mother.

[12]

GETTNER.   Said he would follow
      After? God in heaven, is this the night
      For members of His Imperial Majesty's Government
      To send their young wives on country visits?
      And themselves to follow after? Is he a fool,
      Your good husband? I know the snow tonight
      Comes down as white and soft as a bishop's hand
      But the blessing falls on a night on earth
      When any man's death is right for someone or other.
      Is he a fool, your husband?

GELDA.   Where was my mother
      All through today?

GETTNER.   The roads are very sour
      With men marching. He should know that, dear God.

GELDA. Where was my mother?

BELMANN.   And where were you, Gettner?
      Tell me, who called the Countess out
      On to the very roads you mention. Who
      Was the fool who did it?
      And how do you come to be here? Are you
      Dining with enemies tonight?

GELDA.   Now
      There are no questions I want to ask you, Richard.
      You should know there are friends here, as there always have
          been.

KASSEL. Quite so, Belmann, we don't want this catechism.
      We can be inquisitive by degrees.

BELMANN. I don't agree, Kassel. A man can't know
      How to conduct himself towards another man
      Without the answer to certain basic questions.
      What does the man choose to believe? What good

[13]

And evil has he invented for himself?
In short, how has he made himself exist?
And then, the crux of it all,
Does his chosen existence agree
With the good and evil I invent for myself?
Only then—

KASSEL.   You're being pompous, Belmann.

BELMANN. I choose to be pompous. And will Gettner please
Choose to make his existence plain?

GETTNER.   I think
It's plainer in your words, Belmann, than ever
It would be in mine.

BELMANN.   Will you admit you joined
The Hungarian army?

GETTNER.   Certainly.
It was on a Sunday, between five and six.

BELMANN. Indeed? Then what business have you here?

GETTNER. I was born a casual, unacceptable visitor.

BELMANN. Into what world, it seems, you've never discovered.

KASSEL. Then for heaven's sake be quiet and let him wonder.

BELMANN. We have to make sense of this. We know that arms
Are moving through the night against Vienna.
But here's a stray of the enemy's
Who seems to think he can wander anywhere.

GETTNER. I should never grudge a man
Such a pretty moment of conversion
As I had that Sunday. A wet and windy Sunday.
All the streets were in a holy stupor
Except for the mad bashing of the cathedral bells.
Bash, crash, take that for your damned impudent

Soul, they said: in the name of the Father, the Son,
And the Holy Ghost, bash, bash: we'll lay you
Flat in the mud of Crown Prince Rudolf Street,
You dust. And all I could do for my self-esteem
Was to swear to cherish all hearts that are oppressed;
To give myself to liberty, justice, and the revolution.

STEFAN. And the lynching of Count Latour on Buda bridge.

GETTNER. There are fearful excitements on any side.
Any side can accuse the other
And feel virtuous without the hardships of virtue.
When pride of race has been pent up
In a tyrannous disregard, and valued liberties
Have been lost for long enough, what comes in the way
Of dignity's free and natural flowing
Is nothing but rocks to be blasted. I envy them
Their certainty. Each private man
Has a public cause to elucidate him,
And a reasonable sense of having been wronged.
If you like you can call this man your enemy;
It's what he expects.

BELMANN.   And now, if you like,
Will you tell us how the war goes on without you,
And what interesting manœuvre you've been carrying out today?

Enter the COUNTESS.

COUNTESS. You will not make an interruption of me,
But think I was here from the beginning of the evening;
So I shall know you forgive me.

GELDA. Mother—

JAKOB.   Dear Countess—

KASSEL.   I don't know that I shall
Forgive you, Rosmarin.

[15]

COUNTESS.   Of course you will.
But if all the crooked places of the world
Have been made plain to you while I was out,
That I shall not forgive.

BELMANN.   I assure you, more crooked than ever.

COUNTESS. How few you are. Can so many
Of my friends have died in a week? I was anxious
You should all be astonished to hear
That this morning, by the confusing light
Of one lantern I harnessed the horses, poor angels,
With my own insufficient hands. Will you believe me?

STEFAN. We've already marvelled.

GELDA.   But why did you treat us
As though we cared nothing about you at all?

COUNTESS. Chaffinch, I have to be very vexed with you.
You should not be here; you should be safe in Vienna.

GELDA. But we thought you were lost and dead.

COUNTESS.   Yet when
Have I ever done anything to make you think so?

STEFAN. Why, today you did.

COUNTESS.   Indeed
I am contrite, and very humble, and enchanted
By the perils of the day, because today
I have been as clever as an ostler,
And driven alone, one human and two horses,
Into a redeemed land, uncrossed by any soul
Or sound, and always the falling perfection
Covering where we came, so that the land
Lay perfect behind us, as though we were perpetually
Forgiven the journey. And moreover
A strange prescience possessed me.

[16]

One must have talent to go from a place to a place,
But divination to go so deviously
That north, south, east, and west
Are lost in admiration, and *yet* to arrive,
After a short experience of eternity,
At the place and people one set out to reach:
Namely, to find, in a little farm
Fallen right out of the world in a drift of snow,
Poor hunted Richard.

BELMANN.   Hunted?

GELDA.   Why do you say
Poor hunted Richard?

COUNTESS.   Poor Richard, he is hunted.

KASSEL. Now, Rosmarin, throw some light on this.
No more mystery.

COUNTESS.   Physician dear,
What mystery? Nothing in the world has been hidden,
Only Richard, who has lain for three nights in a barn.

GETTNER. I'm a deserter, simply, I expect
You understand that.

STEFAN.   A deserter, simply!

KASSEL.   Good God!

COUNTESS. Why are you shocked?
He has left them with a whole army but one.
Can they not be perfectly troublesome with that?

BELMANN. In my stupidity I seem to be
One conversion behind. To what dear cause
Are you devoted tonight? What hearts
Do you cherish at present?

[17]

GETTNER. None.
The Hungarians, I see and admire it,
Have a cause, and a passion vigorous enough
To be called a virtue.
But rights exist: causes, faiths, truths,
High thoughts and righteous judgements
Which aren't for me. Boredom and melancholy
Drove me nearly mad.
There's a dreariness in dedicated spirits
That makes the promised land seem older than the fish.

BELMANN. Let me regard him after I've drunk a little.
My glass is empty.

KASSEL. Rosmarin, one thing interests me, when
You set out this morning, how far did you foresee
The danger of your ways? Or, if I may say so,
How well do you realize it even now?

COUNTESS. Little doctor, what do you say to me?
I know the true world, and you know I do.
But we needn't let it think we all bow down.
I haven't forgotten it. Indeed, today
As we turned the horses' heads
I heard the true world singing on the march;
The Hungarian army on the other side of the hill
Sounded like a pack of dogs in cry
To Richard's ears and mine.

STEFAN. I don't know how you tolerate him.
He's a man half-way through his life
With no infirmity except himself,
And yet you let him drag you out
To endure the toughest day, merely
To rescue him from his own feeble fault.

COUNTESS. Nonsense, Stefan. It was all a very simple matter,
  Only complicated by the weather.

GELDA. We know too little to make a judgement yet.
  We should only care
  Richard is out of this unhappy war.
  Here there's no war, Stefan.

KASSEL.   No; but still
  There may be presently. Surely our concern
  Is not whether Gettner should be held responsible
  For the snowfall, or whether or not
  He should have considered the danger and the distance—
  Indeed, he may not have taken into account
  That your mother would circle half round the kingdom—

GETTNER.   Doctor,
  Don't let's give me any imaginary virtues.
  I'd have prayed and begged and bullied her to fetch me
  If the roads had been under fire and water,
  If the distance and the danger had been trebled
  And death not unlikely.
  There was no one else I could believe would come;
  Except the firing-squad, which I was not
  In the mood to welcome.

BELMANN.   I could do its work
  With my own trigger-finger, without a qualm.

GELDA. He sent for help to this house.
  But what help can there ever be for Richard?

KASSEL. Our present concern is whether the Hungarians
  Mean to let you disappear so easily.
  Your name has the ring of reputation,
  And I suppose you may have information

[19]

Which they might think valuable to their success.
And that being so—

GETTNER.   I am infectious, doctor.
You're quite right. I carry the war with me:
None of you can be altogether
Unconcerned, if the Hungarians come
This way, till the army passes with its singing
On to the Vienna road. Until
The snow falls back again to its quiet heaping
Over this house, I'm bound to give you
Great uneasiness. This disease I am
You're all of you guilty of harbouring
Against the liberalities in arms
Who mean to shoot me like a dog. I am sorry
If you should have to take this war seriously.

JAKOB. It's true what he says; Countess, did you think of it?
Suppose they come this way, and suppose by some chance
They know where Gettner's hiding, may it not
Be very unpleasant, most of all for you
Who in your innocence of heart brought him among us?

COUNTESS. Innocent?
I am always perfectly guilty of what I do,
Thank God.

BELMANN.   Countess, you see we're here in a trap
With you and this gentleman of uncertain future.
May we presume to doubt your wisdom and care for us?

JAKOB. No, I never wish to doubt you, Countess,
Nor to hear you doubted! Whatever I reverence
Can be sure of me, as there's a man shall know
On Friday.

BELMANN.   Saturday, I thought.

KASSEL.   Now, now, come along.

COUNTESS. It's very hard to follow you. Saturday you thought,
Or Friday. But I've been lost already
So many times today, it begins to seem
No great misfortune. Let us say
We are all confused, incomprehensible,
Dangerous, contemptible, corrupt,
And in that condition pass the evening
Thankfully and well. In our plain defects
We already know the brotherhood of man.
Who said that?

BELMANN.   You, Countess.

COUNTESS.   How interesting.
I thought it was a quotation.

GELDA.   But the night
Is still a danger for Richard.

JAKOB.   For us, too.

STEFAN. And for Peter, which is worse.
We should send Gettner out into the night again
And let it beat on his own head alone.

GELDA. You don't know what you're saying, Stefan.

STEFAN. I know whose life I value.

GETTNER. For how much longer, I wonder, am I to be
Kept standing in the pillory,
Diagnosed unsatisfactory
By these gentlemen of high soul.
I was never to their liking, nor they to mine
That I can remember,
But perhaps they will agree to let me live
Though it may be some trouble to them. This

[21]

I do know, I'll not die to oblige anybody;
Nor for the sake of keeping up
Decent appearances. Before I do
I'll get down on all fours, foot-kissing,
Dust-licking, belly-crawling,
And any worm can have me for an equal,
Rather than I should have no life at all.

BELMANN. Well, that, I think, is clear.
You have a remarkably short distance to go.

GELDA. Oh, Richard, why do you have to destroy every
Way of coming to you?

GETTNER.   Let me be honest.
I suppose I'm very little else.

GELDA.   I don't know why I should seem
To owe shame to you all for Richard. He is, after all,
His own man, no less if he feels like a child,
And, I know, no care of mine.

STEFAN. Of course he's no care of yours.
Why should he cling round this family, and put
You to shame and mother into danger?

COUNTESS.   So shamefully,
I seem to have gone floating out
Of this interesting present
To some remote evening, a no-man's country.
Now it seems to me very strange
You should all be so occupied in living.

KASSEL. You're not well; you have driven yourself too hard
For too long, Rosmarin.

GELDA.   Darling, you need rest.
Leave us now and get some sleep.

[22]

JAKOB.   Dear Countess—

COUNTESS. No, no, no. It's the perfection of sleep
   To be awake to the dream.
   If I were going to live for ever
   This would be the way: unconcerned
   And yet reasonably fond. I am like an arm or a hand
   After a rigorous long time unflexing.
   It unclenches at last into an apparition
   And touches without feeling
   It is so disenchanted of the body.
   I am altogether so, now that the day is over.
   And I look far back to us all where we are living
   Uncertain people in an uncertain time,
   And it seems long ago. But I confuse you.
   To you the time is close
   And sharp and prevailing. And I shall pray,
   If prayers can make me serious, that tomorrow
   I may concentrate on my responsibilities.
   Till then, for my sake, if my sake is worthy,
   Be like men waiting.

GETTNER. Listen, do you hear that?

KASSEL. Hear what?

JAKOB.   Countess, you heard
   The Hungarian army singing, did you not?

GELDA. Was it like any sound you hear at the moment?
   Listen.

KASSEL. Ah! Then I caught something.

COUNTESS. I am not sure you should listen. If it's the same
   Song that came to us over the hill
   Richard told me it was not proper. But that

Was several hours ago, although of course
If it's very improper perhaps they never get tired of it.

GETTNER. Where are they now?

JAKOB. Not far.

STEFAN. But listen: where's the singing? Surely
It's died away.

JAKOB. But it didn't pass us by.

COUNTESS. Why should it? No one sings for ever.
Let them take breath.

[JAKOB *throws open the window. Military orders are being
shouted some distance away.*

STEFAN. Do you hear that?

GETTNER. They haven't passed the gates.
What Godforgotten bastard saw us
Turn in here, and told them? Now it comes.

COUNTESS. Jakob, do shut the window.
It's very cold. You will give us all pneumonia.

GETTNER. Where shall I go? If they're coming to search the house
Where are you going to hide me? Will you remember
This hour is life and death for me?

GELDA. Do you think
We haven't understood that?

COUNTESS. It is disappointing.
I had begun to be eternally dispassionate,
And life and death at once become the argument.
But don't distrust me, Richard.
I hope I shall do better
Than throw away the gains of the day
To the first indignant animal who comes.

[24]

You can, if you like, climb to the little bell-turret
And draw the rope ladder up after you.
The dirt and spiders and discomfort there
In a filthy way will give the illusion of safety.
But there is still time for nothing to happen.
After all, an army must sometimes halt,
And why not here? Their heels are lumped with snow
And they can kick them clean against my gates
And so march on as light as boys
For a yard or two. Though when I think tonight
May be the last of human time
For some of them, I wish their feet
So very heavy and slow
They could live long lives on the road.

[*A hammering on the outside door. Enter* BELLA.

BELLA.   Madam,
The worst of it is, the house is surrounded by soldiers.
What am I to do about the knocking, madam?

COUNTESS.   If you wish the door
Still to be there to open tomorrow, open it, Bella.

BELLA. Shall I let them in with their guns? If they should ask?

COUNTESS. I believe we can't expect to separate them.

BELLA. They can click their heels at me as much as they like,
They won't make me think it's natural manners.
                                    [*Exit* BELLA.

GETTNER. Who can I trust here? I know I offend
These gentlemen's opinion of the world,
And not one of them cares what becomes of me.

KASSEL. Gettner, Gettner, have some respect for yourself.

GETTNER. Have a respect for my life,

[25]

For the sake of your sleep to come, don't betray me.
Go to your imaginations, gentlemen:
Think of death by shooting.

BELMANN. I should more likely weep for stags or partridges.

COUNTESS. Do, then. Weep for what you can.
It's grateful to our brevity
To weep for what is briefer,
For nothing else will.

GETTNER [*leaning from the landing of the stairs*].
Lie, lie! O Christ, lie for me!

Re-enter BELLA.

BELLA [*closing the door behind her*].
Well, madam, he's a gentleman at least,
And I'm glad to say we know him: Colonel Janik,
Madam, but very peremptory.

COUNTESS.   The geologist!
I remember him; ask him to come in.

BELLA. And what is so strange, I thought I saw
In the dark behind him—

COUNTESS.   But I still think
We'd better not keep him waiting.

BELLA.   Of course it was dark
And there seemed a great many faces, and all with their eyes
Looking straight at me, but there among all those Hungarians—

COUNTESS. Well, Bella, if you will not open the door
I must do it myself.

COLONEL JANIK *comes in without being admitted.*

JANIK.   You will excuse me, Countess.
When there is peace I have more patient manners.

COUNTESS. I remember you with great pleasure, Colonel Janik.

JANIK. Other days, madam, are other days;
I must ask you not to remind me of them.

COUNTESS.   I see
You have something urgent to say to me, Colonel,
And I will not waste your time by asking
Who you know here. I am with my friends and children.

JANIK. I would keep you so, Countess, and all other
Women too. We've been taking a buffeting
Out on the roads. You were sensible
To stay indoors today.

COUNTESS.   You give me credit
For more sense than I can truthfully claim, Colonel.

JANIK. Indeed? It was very courageous of you, Countess
Whatever business forced you out, no doubt
Was harsh and necessary. Any postponement
Was impossible?

COUNTESS.   Colonel, the time is passing.
Perhaps you too have business harsh and necessary.
You mustn't let me be the cause of delay.
We should deny ourselves the pleasure of strategy,
Though I very much admire
How cleverly you invest my position
Under cover of peaceful manœuvre.
But now I think we should have the charge direct.

JANIK. What does the name Captain Gettner
Mean to you, Countess?

COUNTESS.   A fantasy, Colonel.

JANIK. I trusted you to be serious, but I see,
Madam, you mean to play.

[27]

COUNTESS.   I was astonished
For a moment, you must let me be astonished,
Though I should know the world has many surprises
And Richard with a commission might possibly
Be one of them.

JANIK.   I wish I might convey
The pressure of tonight and dawn tomorrow
Which is on my heart,
And ask you, therefore, to respect it.

COUNTESS.   Colonel
You can be certain I do; but you mustn't expect
All men to leave their gentler world for yours.

JANIK. It has been reported that you were seen
With Captain Gettner in your sleigh;
That you apparently brought him to this house.

COUNTESS. It is a house to which I bring my friends.

JANIK. You may not have understood that Captain Gettner
Is a deserter.

COUNTESS.   What else could he possibly be?
Suppose our friend has found himself
No longer bound in understanding to you,
Either in the pursuit of meaning or in any
Wholehearted belief, what except a deserter
Can he possibly be? He might not have supposed
You would let him resign and send him off
With your blessing on his way.

JANIK.   This is a night
For simplicities, madam. I have two thousand men
Standing in the snow, their lives my trust.
Peace may go in search of the one soul
But we are not at peace.

[28]

COUNTESS. *You* are not
  At peace, Colonel.

JANIK.   Captain Gettner
  Has broken his oath to the Hungarian Diet.
  Captain Gettner has deserted in the field.
  Captain Gettner, by the information
  He possesses, has become too threatening
  To my cause and country. For your one man
  I have many, Countess, and I'm here
  To arrest him. If you wish to abide
  By your neutrality, madam, bring him out.
  Otherwise, I regret, we shall come in and find him.

COUNTESS. I have no weapons to prevent you, Colonel.
  The house will go down before you like matchwood.
  Your victory will be complete, if not glorious.
  Though I wonder you should think
  So unhopefully of your own argument
  That you meekly and unmanfully give in
  To violence, when I am ready
  To be persuaded to your opinion
  By any truth which in God's world
  You can put before me. I realize readily
  Time is your anxiety, but in the end
  Who drives the right way drives the fastest,
  As only today I have been reminded.
  I give you one promise: I shall never make
  Myself, or my friends, my way of life
  Or private contentment, or any
  Preference of my nature, an obstacle
  To the needs of a more true and living world
  Than so far I have understood. Only
  Tell me what is in this war you fight

Worth all your dead and suffering men.
Your faith is, your country has been refused
Its good rights, for many years too long.
So be certain, whatever the temptation,
No man is made a slave by you.
To you Austria is a tyranny.
Then, to the number of those men who die,
And far beyond that number infinitely,
Surely you will show
One man over another has no kingdom.
Otherwise, how shall I understand your war?
Because I have respect for Richard Gettner's
Wandering and uncertain will, *therefore*
I have respect for your sheer purpose
And for those many men I cannot
Know by name who are waiting in the snow.
But if you tell me Richard Gettner
Has thrown away his claim to freedom
By claiming that a man is free, then you
And those in the snow, may as well march
Against your guns and swords. They are tyrannous, too.
Is it not a quaint freedom, that lets us
Make up our minds and not be free to change them?
Poor hope for me! I change my mind
For pure relaxation, two or three times a day,
As I get wiser or sillier, whichever it is I do.
Must I save your cause for you, Colonel?
If so, then not in my name or Richard Gettner's
But in the name of all your nameless fellows
Who trust their suffering is righteous
I forbid you to invade the liberties of this house.

JANIK. For your sake, madam, I would love
Anarchy if I could. To search this house

And your estate will be a dangerous delay for us.
Instead, I offer you a free choice.
I have someone with me under my charge
Who may help us to a peaceful understanding.

> [*He opens the door.*]

Corporal, give Count Zichy my compliments
And ask him to be kind enough to let us have his company.

STEFAN. Peter! Now what damage have I done?

GELDA. What do they do with Peter?

BELMANN. Is this quite in good warfare, Colonel,
To have taken prisoner a civilian
Of such distinction, going about his peaceful
Business?

JANIK.   If I were you, sir, I should not
Draw my attention to you.

> *Enter* COUNT PETER.

GELDA.   Peter blessed,
What has happened?

PETER.   They were at the gate to welcome me.

JANIK. Count Zichy, we need you to show us the way to agree.

PETER. In this house we have always agreed fairly enough, Colonel.
You have your field of war; you should keep to it.

COUNTESS. But I have enlarged it to include myself,
Peter, so the Colonel tells me. Alas,
Peter, I am hotly debatable ground.

STEFAN. Peter, I brought this on you.

PETER.   No such thing;
Time and place have conspired against us.

[31]

JANIK. That is one conspiracy for another,
  And of the two it seems the fairer. So,
  Countess, time and place give you a choice;
  If you give up Gettner to answer for himself,
  We free Count Zichy, and no further action
  Is taken against this house.
  Or the Count remains our prisoner and marches with us.
  By bringing Gettner to this house, to meet the Count
  And pass his information to the government,
  You have done worse by us, I hope
  Your goodness tells you, than we are doing to you.

STEFAN. Wrong!

COUNTESS.   You are wrong.

GELDA.   No such thing could happen.

STEFAN. Wrong, wrong, Colonel! It was all
  A ridiculous chance. I sent for the Count
  Only because I was afraid for my mother.

JANIK.   That
  May be, I don't know, but we're not without the danger.
  Choose, Countess. My men are in the cold.
  It is time you gave us Gettner, and let us go.

COUNTESS. Colonel, no man is mine to give you.

PETER. Bargaining with family affection, Colonel,
  Isn't war. As I know this house, you have my word
  There's been no conspiracy.

JANIK.   So on your word
  My men can pride themselves, as they go into battle,
  That I failed to lead them even to the arrest
  Of one deserter from the hands of a woman
  Because of the word of the Emperor's Government.

[32]

Sir, for many centuries we have been able
To judge the word of the Emperor's Government.

PETER. You should know I love Hungary.

JANIK. I know that you're Hungarian. I know
Your voice in the Austrian Council must of course
Be moderate. I do not know
You love Hungary.

PETER.   How shall I tell you
I love Hungary? Your love goes to war,
Mine stays at home, and there's no comparison:
You march with Buda-Pesth, and I reason with Vienna.
You have the benefit of passion, Colonel:
The world can see you with your life held high
Ready to hurl it out of your living hand
For the sake of Hungary, even perhaps
To lose the life of Hungary, too; and Hungary loves you.
Whereas, whatever I wish, in fact I see
Hungary's best future in Austria's friendship,
And I remain, if you like, the fool
Of my own faith and fallibility,
And Hungary scorns me; there's no comparison.
I see you love Hungary, I think it may be
To Hungary's sorrow. For me, there's nothing to show;
But indeed there can be love without evidence.

JANIK. Yes, yes; you're perfectly sincere,
You will always do what you can;
We're not ungrateful for your interest.
Count Zichy; it's only a pity
There's no better world fit to receive it.
But, excuse me, I think even in your world of paper
Desertion in the field has consequences.
Isn't it so?

[33]

PETER.   It is so.

JANIK.   Choose, Countess.

COUNTESS. There is no choice.

STEFAN No, there's no choice. By our fault
And his good nature, Peter's a prisoner.
And we're prisoners in Peter until he's free.
There's no question of choosing.

JANIK.   Well, then, Countess.

COUNTESS. You put me very near the hard heart of the world,
Colonel, where bad and good eat at the same table.
No man is mine to give you.

STEFAN.   Will you give him
Peter, then? Eyes of God,
Will you give him Peter?

COUNTESS.   I may never know
What it is I do in the eyes of God.

STEFAN. Will someone less than God, and more than me,
Tell my mother what she is doing? Doctor
Kassel, will you tell her?

PETER.   Stefan,
As less than God and more than you, I tell you
To hold your tongue. Deep water is for those
Who can swim.

STEFAN.   I see.

KASSEL. Still, if I thought you wanted another opinion,
Rosmarin, I should give my opinion against you.

BELMANN. Philosophically, Countess, you may be reasonable,
But humanly I see no point of balance
Between a man and a rat.

JAKOB.   There's no
    Faith in Gettner, that's evident: I see
    No doubt of which of the two is worthy.
    I can't believe in a spiritual democracy.

BELMANN. Countess, when Jakob and I agree
    It is time to consider.

COUNTESS.   I have your own words, Peter,
    For my comfort; there can be love without evidence.
    No one can know how unwillingly I fail you,
    But if it could be known, you of all men
    Should know it. I believe
    And witness you love Hungary, though in these times
    You make yourself separate as an enemy.
    Will you believe of me
    That I decide against my love
    With as much distress?

PETER.   I hope I do:
    I know I do, with what humility I have,
    And I wish there were no conceit in me
    To let me bid myself against another man.

JANIK. You must excuse me, Count Zichy, but I have
    To ask you to leave with me. It isn't the way
    I should wish to bring you among your countrymen,
    But you come among them, and even that
    I incline to welcome. Come, now.

STEFAN. Gelda—you fetch Gettner here!
    You're the only one of us now
    Who may persuade him.

JAKOB.   That's true, certainly.
    Not even Gettner would harden his heart against you.

BELMANN. Well, we shall see. For myself, I have
   A less heroic opinion of him.

STEFAN.   So, Gelda,
   Go to him, find him, plead with him.
   Colonel, I assure you—my sister will bring Gettner.

GELDA. Make my mother go, who brought him here.

STEFAN. You know my mother has refused. You have
   The best right to go. Peter's your husband.

GELDA. Richard was my husband.

STEFAN.   Gelda! What are you saying?

GELDA. You know Richard was my husband; though
   It was only in a word, but still a word
   Stays in the mind and has its children too.
   I am Peter's wife, and everything
   Is so well with us, our marriage vows
   Go on like dancers, with no thought in the world to carry,
   Only to be as easy and loving as we are.
   But I was Richard's wife, and those vows,
   Though they're cancelled and nowhere now,
   Were abounding in purpose then, looking ahead
   With eyes narrowed against the weather
   To make a way where there was no way.
   By which anxious journey we might have progressed
   Beyond our selves to ourselves made wiser.
   But we wouldn't venture.
   Peter, if you rest in our love as I do,
   Don't wish me to ask Richard to die.

PETER. There's no fear of that; no one need ever die
   For us; you know I understand.
   My God, I should be sorry to see
   A dead man cross our love. Why, it's as much

[36]

For us as for him that you refuse to persuade him.
So say good-bye, with clear hearts, both of us.
In the order of things, when events will have it,
I shall come stolidly home.
We shall think nothing of this presently.

JANIK. Count Zichy.

PETER.   Coming.

COUNTESS.   Colonel Geologist,
You would do better to love your rocks and ammonites
Than flog your heart with your fellow countrymen.
You have such a dangerous, partial love.
Guard you, Peter.

PETER.   Guard you, Rosmarin.

GELDA. What am I doing, Peter?

PETER.   There's nothing
You need to wonder. All goes well.

> [*He goes through the door.* JANIK *salutes and follows him.*
> *A pause.*

STEFAN. He didn't look at me. He knows
I brought this on him.

BELMANN. If ever there was a bad exchange we've seen it now.
I feel indignant and aggrieved.

KASSEL.   And I seriously wonder
Whether the drive you took so far in the snow,
Rosmarin, is finished even yet.

BELMANN. No good can come of it.

JAKOB. No good will ever come of Gettner.

COUNTESS. That may be true.

> [STEFAN *opens the window. They hear the shouting of*
> *military commands as the* COUNTESS *goes up the stairs.*

THE CURTAIN FALLS

[37]

ACT TWO

The stables

GETTNER *is standing on a manger looking through a small, high, round window. The sound of a door opening and shutting. GETTNER jumps off the manger and runs across to a ladder leading up to a loft. In each side-pocket he carries a bottle. Enter* STEFAN.

STEFAN. You don't have to run away from me particularly.
    I've never had a reason to be
    Anything but harmless. I saw you coming
    Across the yard to the stables; fortunately
    The Hungarians were too concerned with themselves
    To notice.

GETTNER. What have they come back for?

STEFAN.   Not for you.

GETTNER. I didn't think so. But I suppose
    Something brought them.

STEFAN.   Apparently they've come
    To lick their wounds. They had a surprise encounter
    With a wandering regiment of Austrian Dragoons,
    Not the battle either of them was expecting.
    They rounded a corner and came face to face
    And were startled into a fight. They hurt each other
    And both sides have retired to look it up
    In Heister's *Tactics and Military Manœuvre*.

GETTNER. How long do they think they're going to stay here?
    How long do you think a man can bear
    To be shot through the head by every slamming door he hears?

[38]

Purgatory, why do they have to choose
This place to come to?

STEFAN.   At your invitation.
I should say it's a natural choice
Since this house became a pocket of the war.
They have a good many wounded, and some dead.
But Peter isn't one of them, if that
Should interest you.

GETTNER.   That's something I don't need
To take the blame for. What else is on your mind?
I should suppose no dog-like devotion
Made you follow me in here.

STEFAN.   I have to see you
To believe you. How else can I imagine
A man so without benefit to anybody?

GETTNER. Ah, yes; how? How indeed? Or alternatively
I can sleep and dream dreams of good sense
And wake to find the world is past belief.
Either way, imagination's useless.

STEFAN. I wish you would give me the cue for peace.
Maybe I've a lazy temper; certainly
I dislike disliking. You just have to show me
Where you keep your sympathy
For the people I've most affection for,
And I'll understand if I can. How much
Do you care for my mother?

GETTNER.   There's no one on earth
I would put to more trouble.

STEFAN.   You're succeeding. Already
Her house and her quiet have gone. You set
Great store by your life. What secret value has it
Which makes you claim so much for keeping it?

[39]

GETTNER. Unless I live, how do you think I can know?

STEFAN. Suppose its value should be the chance to die
At the right moment?

GETTNER.   That's an assumption
Very difficult afterwards to verify.

STEFAN. But if I ever thought we should give you up
I don't think so now. Whole armies might dissolve
For the same reason, but even so, if you honestly
Change step in your mind, I fail to see
How to condemn you. But was it honestly?
Or are my family suffering to let you play?
I have to know before I can be at all easy;
So to make the matter clear would you be ready
To risk your life if I give you the opportunity?

GETTNER. I don't know what the hell you're talking about.

STEFAN. I won't stand to see my family
Made miserable to save a coward, if a coward
Is what you are. You'd honour yourself and me
By exchanging shots at twenty paces.

GETTNER.   Should I so?
I'll honour myself by continuing to live,
And honour you by hoping you live indefinitely.

STEFAN. My chance of killing you would be infinitesimal.
I'm no great shot.

GETTNER.   Don't be an idiot.
How shall I add to the pleasures of your family
By waving a pistol at you? My boy, you think
Too poorly of me. I would never
Trouble a soul beyond my own small needs.
And I possess enough honour, I might say,

[40]

To remain dishonoured without indignation.—
Who's that?

Enter GELDA.

STEFAN.   You caught him on the nerve.

GELDA. Poor Richard; we breathed again too soon.
Poor Richard; but none of us can feel
Much favoured by the event. God bless
My grandfather, who thought no building made
By human hands could be too good for horses.

STEFAN. Why, particularly?

GELDA.   Because here we have to make
Our home until the Hungarians go. The house
Is hospital, headquarters, barracks,
Armoury, pandemonium.
In the middle of the swarm, immovable
As a queen bee, our mother is standing
Fascinated and appalled.
When I speak she stares at me a moment
As though she couldn't grasp what language I spoke in,
And then turns away, and sometimes
Gasps and claps her hands
Like a little girl at a circus. Do
Bring her away, Stefan. You might persuade her.
I think without knowing it she may break her heart.

STEFAN. I think she may.

[Exit STEFAN.

GELDA.   Where will you go to be safe?

GETTNER. The possibilities aren't many. Where else
Except here in the loft?

GELDA.   It can't be for long:
Perhaps a day.

[41]

GETTNER.   Not long: perhaps a day!
  Only a child could think tomorrow
  As far off as it seems to me.
  But a child can sleep, and I can court
  Insensibility. It is a splendid mercy
  The mind needn't be nakȩd for too long.

GELDA. And not feel the naked world, or who
  Goes through it. It is a way, certainly.
  You made such an outcry about life yesterday
  I thought you meant more than undisturbed breathing.
  But as I've never been in fear of death
  I've no right to question what you do.

GETTNER.   No, none;
  Though I can tell you, fear as an experience
  Is remarkably unenlightening.
  What does your young brother mean to do?

GELDA. What should he do?

GETTNER.   You perfect and upright family.
  I'll go to my wallow where the apples are rotten.
        [*He begins to climb the ladder to the loft. He puts his fore-
         head against a rung.*
  I don't trust him.

GELDA.   No, why should you?
  Why should you trust anyone? It's unlikely
  You can draw from the world what you never paid into it.
  Some people doubt most what they lack most.
  Are we to trust you, is my mother to trust you
  To keep her from harm?

GETTNER. No, by God, she's beyond harm.
  And I'm beyond help, I remember you said.
  But my simple nature asks better of men
  Than I should ever presume to provide.

[42]

GELDA.   So far
Wouldn't you say we've answered you? With a shade
Of suffering.

GETTNER.   You have. Your mother
Pitched the night on a heroic level.
But now we have come to the drudgery of heroism.
So far you've spoken. But now's the time
When you have to drag out the plain length
Of your magnificent word. I'm only wondering.
The good husband is still among us.

GELDA.   Yes,
I know. We've been given the chance to think again.

GETTNER. I'm interested, naturally.
We have to be prepared; first thoughts
Have shallow roots, I imagine.

GELDA.   Be reassured.
It's also Peter's wish we should keep you safe.

GETTNER. Is it, by Peter? Then, by Peter, he shows
A very praiseworthy nobility.
And you? You will hardly think the bargain bearable.
You're deeply regretting it.

GELDA.   I think neither
Of deep regrets nor of no regrets. You
Are the only gainer, Richard, so be grateful.

GETTNER. Isn't a man to know the reason
For his salvation? I give my gratitude
To what I understand. You wouldn't endure
Being praised for what, after all, may be
A whim of the moment. Come, now, Gelda;
I've some hours to spend in solitary thought,

And I should be happier if all the devil doubts
Could be exorcised.

GELDA.   Very well, I'll tell you.
I was a failure to you once. I know
No more about that than I did. But now
In the simpler matter of guarding you
I shall try not to fail.

GETTNER.   Is there another
Word in the language so unnecessary
As 'fail' or 'failure'?
No one has ever failed to fail in the end:
And for the very evident reason
That we're made in no fit proportion
To the universal occasion; which, as all
Children, poets, and myth-makers know,
Was made to be inhabited
By giants, fiends, and angels of such size
The whole volume of human generations
Could be cupped in their hands;
And very ludicrous it is to see us,
With no more than enough spirit to pray with,
If as much, swarming under gigantic
Stars and spaces. In this insecure
Situation, I found from the first,
Your mother managed to find a stability
Beside which any despair was compelled to hesitate:
And I was half caught in an expectation of life
Which she was good enough to show no sign
Of expecting from me.
But then—in the way a good hostess
Brings to your notice a fine possession
Without precisely pointing to it—

[44]

She made me aware of you;
And to root myself in her radiance
I married you. What did she mean by it?
It was the kind of mockery I knew
So well.

GELDA.   Why do you say that? Who mocked you?

GETTNER. You may remember I tried to handle
My native language; in the vain belief
It would give way to me and let me
Turn it to my uses.

GELDA.   No one mocked you then.

GETTNER. Reality itself, with wonder and power,
Calls for the sound of great spirits
And mocks us with a wretched human capacity.
Each day has shone full on me. I have senses,
Nerves, and mind. Out of this conjunction
One would suppose there might be born
Words nearly like the world. Yet no;
I wrote frustration syllable by syllable.—
I beg your pardon, it was you
We were talking about. There you were,
Rambling your way out of childhood,
Not knowing what innocence was, being innocent,
And, in a way, perfect in your imperfection.
I don't know how I was expected
To pair with that, unless I was willing
To be the misfortune around the house,
The disappointer of expectations,
Affecting virtue so that I should not see
The shadow go across you.
I preferred to remain unracked, as I preferred
To stay silent, since it wasn't for me

To recreate one word fit to stand
Beside reality, unhumiliated.
And therefore, with mockery refused,
Failure hardly presents itself.

GELDA. Yours may not, but mine may. I meant
To love you. Moreover, I meant I should be loved.
Solemnly to God I said so.

GETTNER.   Quite so.
But when promises are merely hopes, and hopes
Aren't realized, where are the promises kept?

GELDA. In me, it would seem.

GETTNER.   I see. And I see as well
Strange possibilities.

GELDA.   You needn't think
I shall take less care for your safety than I would
If I were still your wife.

GETTNER.   You can now tell me
Why you talk to me like this? With no
Confidence at all, I'm bound to ask you
Am I loved in any way? I know I'm not,
But, for my own good, I should like
This conversation well defined.

GELDA.   Richard,
There's no definition. I was turning back
To some old thoughts. Some sort of love there was,
But whether it left me or whether I turned from it
It became remote. Sometimes
You can watch a single bird flying over
Towards the vague mountains, until you no longer know
Whether you see or imagine where it is.
I have a feeling of no definition.

[46]

GETTNER. I am a man to be loved, is in her mind;
    God listen to that, a man to be loved,
    She almost says so, as a general theory.
    In a world of exact and well-founded husbands
    Gettner appears wifeworthy. Be very careful
    Or you'll have me wooing my way backwards
    To the chancel of All Angels 1838.—
    To return you fair for fair,
    Now that you're a woman of uncertain mind,
    For whom sin and virtue are both
    Equally undefinable, I see
    You might be loved, more than sufferably.
    With the greatest respect, I entertain you
    As husbandworthy.

GELDA.   If what I said
    Turns into that for you, it wasn't worth saying.
    I meant that you should lie in hiding
    Not altogether alone with fear, and have
    A faith in faith, of some sort. But I know
    Foreign tongues are as many as human beings
    And not easy to translate. Whatever I said
    Can be forgotten.

GETTNER.   No phrase makes memory
    More certain. I like this language, full
    Of yes-no and no-yes, and a faith
    Which I'm to have and not to have, and things
    Which have been but not yet. It belongs
    To the origins and life of sense;
    All my senses tremble. But if you think
    Silence is the better speech
    We can kiss without a word,

[47]

A dead husband and a dead wife
Perpetuated in a sacrament.

GELDA. The dead may have a thought, but no more deeds.

GETTNER. Now which of us has the fear?
You may have withdrawn the words, but they implied
A kindness which you can't help leaving with me,
Which has to be confirmed. My curiosity
Is great; I begin to wonder who you are.

[*He kisses her.*

How dead are the husband and the wife? No words, now.
And yet I also wonder how it must feel
To be so close to a living body
Which in a question of hours may well
Be dead, gone, and promising to be rotten?

GELDA. Why won't you be fair? You cheat and cheat.
Be good to me.

[*They kiss again, and stand apart.*

GETTNER.   You were quite right to remember
I married you. It was time I should be reminded.

GELDA. Was it?

GETTNER.   The human arms can seem
A great security, for the time they hold.
Pathetically, since they secure nothing.
Nevertheless, it was what you meant.

GELDA. Nevertheless, it could perhaps have been what I meant.

GETTNER. I'm extremely grateful.

Enter STEFAN.

STEFAN.   Gettner, if you still
Want to save yourself for better things,
Make yourself scarce. The Hungarians are coming,

[48]

Or at least three of them,
And my mother and the Colonel close behind.
The house is given up; you may as well
Be kept. Trouble had better have a cause.

GELDA. Thank you, Stefan.

STEFAN.   Did you think I wouldn't warn you?

GELDA. Why, no, but—

STEFAN.   Have you really any reason to thank me?

GETTNER [*climbing the ladder*].
Ask him what better thing it is he thinks
I should save myself for? Put it to him.

GELDA. For your own sake is enough.

GETTER [*looking from the loft*].   Don't let me starve.

GELDA. We're not likely to forget you.—Nor remember
Too much the worst of him, Stefan. What was it
He meant me to ask you?

STEFAN.   I was hoping
For the best of him. But it's something I haven't got
An answer to, not yet; though I still may get one.

        [*Enter* BELLA *and* WILLI *with supplies, and* HUNGARIAN
        SOLDIERS *carrying furniture*.
                                    [*Exit* STEFAN.

BELLA. You so much as graze it, you'll carry the mark the rest
of your life. And choose what you grumble at. You've never
been so near to glory as being allowed to have that in your
hands, you poor brute creatures, let me say.

1ST SOLDIER. Put it down, Gyuri. She's swearing at us. March all
night in the flaking snow, fight all morning in the flaking snow,
and then go on fatigues and not flaking grumble. Don't be
ridiculous.

[49]

BELLA. You can't tell the difference between good and bad. You give your eyes to this, now; it was made many, many years ago with wonderful love and care.

1ST S. So was I, but who's carrying me?

BELLA. I won't waste my time. No, Willi, wipe those tears off your face. Haven't you seen madam is laughing, though never so sad in her life?

WILLI. I want to be a soldier, mam.

BELLA. What, a soldier like these bad men? Bad, abominable men.

2ND S. That's all right, ma. You just tell us what to do before we go and sit down.

3RD S. Make the most of your attitudes. Here's god almighty.

1ST S. Tell him we're not wanting anything.

BELLA. And madam homeless.

    [*Enter the* COUNTESS *and* COLONEL JANIK. *The* SOLDIERS *salute.*

COUNTESS. You shall see, Colonel, it is only a little hardship.
You may put me out of your mind, as you put me out of my house:
I shall find employment.

JANIK.   Continue, men.

3RD S.   Sir.

BELLA. Don't be dismayed, madam. I promise you
They shall handle each thing as though it was myself.

1ST S. Disaster.

JANIK.   Get on with your work.

1ST S.   Sir!

COUNTESS. And the good soldiers, Bella, take care of them.
They're being put to so much trouble.

BELLA. Who started it, madam?

[*Exeunt* BELLA, SOLDIERS, *and* WILLI.

COUNTESS.   A lot of time would be wasted
Going back through the years to answer that.
We could scarcely be of our own time if we would,
Being moved about by such very old disturbances.
If we could wake each morning with no memory
Of living before we went to sleep, we might
Arrive at a faultless day, once in a great many.
But the hardest frost of a year
Will not arrest the growing world
As blame and the memory of wrong will do.

JANIK. Then you have no thought for the downtrodden men,
The overlong injustice, madam?

COUNTESS.   Not
As they are downtrodden, but as they are men
I think of them, as they should think of those
Who oppress them. We gain so little by the change
When the downtrodden in their turn tread down.
But then, deserters all, we should all change sides,
I dare say; and that would be proper behaviour
For a changeable world, and no more tiring
Than to go to the extraordinary lengths
Which men will go to, to be identical
Each day. I'm not sure, Colonel, whether I think
Of you as a foe or a friend.
You put me under pain of enmity
And have driven me out of my possessions,
And yet this exile, though it is
No more than a stable-yard from home,

[51]

Unites me with you, and with your soldiers
Who are so willing to die
For what death will take away from them.
You teach me to let the world go, Colonel.
I've known this house so long,
Loved it so well
The hours, as they came and went, were my own people.
In obedience, time never failed me, as though
The keys of the year were on my chatelaine.
Summer would end, surely, but the year fell
For my sake, dying the golden death
As though it were the game to put
Hands over my eyes and part them suddenly
When primroses and violets lay
Like raindrops on a leaf
In the beginning of Spring.
The years occupied themselves about me.
The house was perpetual; it was the stars
Which turned and fled. You see how well you have done
To remind me my only privilege
Was to go about a vanishing garden.

JANIK. Countess, madam, you will excuse me;
But I'll kiss your hand, if I may;
Countess, for God's sake, if you'll permit me.

GELDA. Can you ask that, Colonel, ask for a kindness
While you still mean to be unkind?

COUNTESS. To one as poorly circumstanced as I am
It is most considerate and friendly.

[JANIK *kisses her hand.*

Now, I am sure, you must go back to your mischief.

JANIK. It may seem to you a poor sort of divided man
Who stops to apologize in the course of action;

[52]

But apology isn't repentance. I have to find
A new heart for these men, in a few hours.
They have ahead of them a day
When their spirit will be worth a nation.
To take your house is bully's work, certainly,
But it has a slight flavour of victory for them
To offset the day's mishap. And two or three
May die tonight more of a Christian death
For the blessing of a roof. You gave
A thousand bodies unexpected comfort
When you put yourself at odds with us yesterday.

COUNTESS. Then I give it again, voluntarily.
But if my behaviour gave you this, then so
Did Richard Gettner's. You will have to acknowledge
The real provoker of your good. Desertion,
As you generously admit, has now
Changed into benefit. You will want to give
Richard Gettner his liberty to do
More good with.

JANIK.   That, madam, is woman's logic.
The facts are exactly as they were.

COUNTESS. Facts? Bones, Colonel. The skeleton
I've seen dangling in the School of Anatomy
Is made of facts. But any one of the students
Makes the skeleton look like a perfect stranger.
Richard's fact, in your military law,
Is guilty of death. But Richard's reality
Is making its own way on its own ground,
And only *seems* to take its place in your war.
You can think he is executed already
And entered already into a future life
As a civilian.

[53]

JANIK.   It passes my understanding
    What you imagine you champion in this man?
    I see no hope of any outcome
    Except the disturbing of your own peace.

COUNTESS. Life has a hope of him
    Or he would never have lived. Colonel,
    Can you prophesy the outcome of your war?
    Yet you still go about it. Richard lives
    In his own right, Colonel, not in yours
    Or mine.

JANIK.   I've said I don't intend
    To search for him; but keep him out of my way.

COUNTESS. I shall do what I can to help you.
    And then my son-in-law, am I not to see him?
    Will he not visit me in exile?

JANIK.   You make
    Light of the ways of war, Countess.

COUNTESS.   I take them
    Seriously. And therefore I suppose them
    Reasonable, sensible, and civilized.
    And therefore I cannot see
    Why I should not be allowed to speak to my son-in-law.

JANIK. Well, you shall. I'll send him to you.
    But his guard will stay beside him.

COUNTESS.   Thank you, Colonel.
    We shall give you no trouble. We shall be as you trust us.

                              [JANIK *salutes and goes.*

    I hope I'm not a distraction to providence,
    But I seem to be almost undoing
    The events of yesterday.

[54]

GELDA.   Almost
  Is a far cry.

COUNTESS.   What would you wish to do?
  Never to have known the events of yesterday,
  Or to have used them differently?

GELDA.   For your sake,
  Remembering this outcome, never to have known them.
  For Peter's sake, never to have known them.
  For Richard's sake, could I have used them differently?
  For my sake—I don't know how to answer.
  Questions I've not known I was asking
  Have appeared in fact, as though I called them.

COUNTESS. You've never in all these years questioned
  Why I didn't protect you from marrying Richard.

GELDA [glancing at the loft].
  No. No, I haven't questioned it.

COUNTESS. I sometimes wished you would. Haven't you
  Sometimes thought I took no care of you?

GELDA. It was long ago; we won't think of it now.
  I wanted to marry Richard.

COUNTESS.   There was then
  The glow still about him, from having been
  The momentary genius of the day,
  And there he was unclaimed and difficult,
  Charming to a little girl. And there was I
  Who guessed it wouldn't be easy.

GELDA. Please don't talk of it now.

COUNTESS.   I let you
  Marry Richard, though I knew you would find
  Happiness only by a fine shade,
  Or in some special sense of happiness,

Or not at all. But whoever you had chosen
I couldn't be sure they would cherish you:
And I knew you were prepared that loving Richard
Might be a heavy devotion and a long
Experience of daring. That seemed your purpose;
And I had a pride to see you go
To such a task of love. I knew
Richard was no brute, and no
Pursuer of evil, but more like one enraged
Because he thought that good rejected him.
Or as if an instrument were lying
Thrummed by the wind, refusing any hands
Which might molest the strings into a true sound.

    [GETTNER *laughs in the loft. The* COUNTESS *hears him,*
       and raises her voice a little.

Richard sometimes reminds me of an unhappy
Gentleman, who comes to the shore
Of a January sea, heroically
Strips to swim, and then seems powerless
To advance or retire, either to take the shock
Of the water or to immerse himself again
In his warm clothes, and so stands cursing
The sea, the air, the season, anything
Except himself, as blue as a plucked goose.
It would be very well if he would one day
Plunge, or dress himself again.

GELDA. That isn't the parable to comfort us
On a winter night!

    Enter BELMANN *and* JAKOB *carrying a picture.*

COUNTESS.   I shall find my spirits again.
Here we are, bringing western culture to the horses.
I've never colonized before.

BELMANN.   I should like it
    To be understood that by helping Jakob to carry
    This picture I haven't agreed with him in the least
    About its merits. He is carrying it
    To protect it from possible destruction.
    I am carrying it to protect the soldiers
    From certain corruption of taste. Where
    Is the darkest corner?

JAKOB.   I sometimes think
    His critical judgement is so exquisite
    It leaves us nothing to admire except his opinion.
    He should take into account
    The creative value of the fault.

                    Enter STEFAN.

BELMANN. Hey, hi, ho! You astonish me.
    When I made that precise point yesterday,
    You found it such a blinding blow to your honour
    You had to challenge me.

JAKOB.   A personal matter.
    You haven't the right to mention it here.

COUNTESS. I think he should be allowed to mention it;
    It may be interesting.

JAKOB.   No, really, I must refuse—

BELMANN. It redounds to his credit, and concerns you, Countess.

COUNTESS. So you see, it is interesting.

BELMANN.   I said in your absence,
    There were things you had done which were arguably
    Reprehensible.

COUNTESS.   You showed yourself
    A master of the obvious. And Jakob

[57]

Rightly challenged you for describing me
With such little wit. If his rapier has
No better point, Jakob, you can receive it
On a wide front, and come back to play patience with me.

STEFAN [*to* JAKOB]. Did you really challenge him for that?

JAKOB. As a matter of fact, I'm very worried
About the whole affair.

BELMANN.   Ah! You have only
To say so, my dear fellow, I shall excuse you.

JAKOB. I'm not climbing down, nothing of the sort.
What was a point of honour yesterday
Is, of course, a point of honour today.
My concern is that if I should have the misfortune
To kill you—

BELMANN.   My concern, surely?

JAKOB. But what faith do you possess, to regard your death
In the light of? Just suppose this affair
Should deliver you up, like a deserter, to
An eternity of reparation?
It kept me awake last night.

BELMANN.   Very civil of you.
So perhaps you would like to withdraw?

JAKOB.   No,
I should not like to withdraw. It's very
Annoying of you to suggest I should.
But you can assure me first, you're not entirely
Unaware of your soul's journey.

BELMANN.   I can't
Assure you. You're being quite impossible.
Now when I tell you I've no particular
Belief in my immortal soul

[58]

You will say I'm glad of the excuse
To avoid defending my integrity.
And if, to quieten your scruples, I assume
The appearance of faith, I shall have no integrity
To defend.

JAKOB.   That's perfectly true.

BELMANN.   And I shall say
You've thought of this for no better reason
Than to get out of the whole affair.

JAKOB.   It's not so!
I deny that, absolutely.

COUNTESS.   I can see
Nothing will ever happen to either of you.

        Enter PETER, *with* TWO HUNGARIAN GUARDS.

GELDA. Peter!

STEFAN.   Peter, they swore to me
You were unhurt.

PETER.   As they think of wounds,
I am. And I brought this on myself.
In the fight with the Austrian dragoons this morning
I became the very passion I opposed, and was glad to be.
I borrowed a sword out of someone's useless hand,
And as long as the fighting lasted
I was, heart and soul, the revolution.
Janik thought he had won me over,
But on the way back I convinced him otherwise.

STEFAN. You fought for them? I don't understand.
I've never known you to waver yet.

PETER.   I suppose
There's no balance without the possibility
Of overbalancing.

STEFAN.　　　　　　What shall we do?
　How are we going to set you free of them?

1ST GUARD. We don't stand by for any such talk as that.

COUNTESS. No, you shall not; but you shall sit by me
　And have any talk you choose. Are you
　Military by nature or misfortune?

1ST GUARD. Well, ma'am—

2ND GUARD. Better say nature. You've heard of nature.
　It's us, Rusti.

PETER.　　　　　　It isn't so easy, Stefan.
　I don't know at the moment how I can want
　To be free of these fellows. I'm no less convinced
　Than I always was, they're doing themselves a wrong,
　And doing as great a damage to Hungary
　As to Austria. But I know it now
　In a different sense. I can taste it
　Like a fault of my own, which is not the same
　Flavour as the fault of some other man.
　Besides, I know already from today's showing
　That when they fail,
　If they do fail and head for defeat,
　Being in the heart of their disaster
　Makes it more difficult to leave them.
　It's an odd chance, Rosmarin,
　But your fetching Gettner in
　Has faced me with a knowledge I was lacking,
　Which in a way has altered nothing
　And altered it thoroughly.

BELMANN. May I venture to point out to you, Jakob,
　The truth of what I was saying yesterday?
　How, as I said, how apparently

[60]

Undemandingly the Countess moves among us:
And yet lives make and unmake themselves
In her neighbourhood as nowhere else.

COUNTESS. If, as well as turning a fine phrase,
You also spoke the truth, how proud of you
We all should be.

BELMANN. Thank you my dear Countess.
Yet I'll wager you, Jakob:
One man the Countess will never change
By her divine non-interference:
Ten kronen against Gettner's chances.

JAKOB. Your stable behaviour, I imagine.

COUNTESS. We're continually coming together, as though to live
Pleasantly in one another's conversation,
And each time we find ourselves distracted
By what is happening to us. Do let us
For a short while abandon incident
And charm ourselves with something quite immaterial.

1ST GUARD. I don't know whether you would be interested,
Ma'am, to see a letter from my wife?

COUNTESS. Yes, indeed. How kind of you to show me,
And how the handwriting puts mine entirely to shame.

1ST GUARD. I can't say whose that would be, ma'am.
But you see at the bottom it says 'Your dear wife Anna'.
Those would be her own words, ma'am.
        [GETTNER *starts to climb down the ladder from the loft.*

BELMANN. I won't even turn my eyes in the direction
Of what I've seen. No one can say
I'm responsible for anything that follows.

JAKOB. If it's faith you're discussing—

BELMANN. It isn't. No one can say I made any indication.
I'm not responsible for anything that follows.

GELDA [*whispering urgently at the foot of the ladder*].
Go back, go back, Richard!

JAKOB.   Gettner!

1ST GUARD. Who's this, then? By jankers, I see who it is!

2ND GUARD. By jankers, do you see who it is?

COUNTESS.   Jump
To no conclusions. There's no haste for judgement.
We can make up our minds over a number of years.

1ST GUARD. We've something we know what to do, here.

PETER.   Your Colonel
Made a different bargain, Corporal.

COUNTESS. What has brought you to us, Richard?

GETTNER [*full of drink, but carrying it very fairly*].
I was ignored up there. You can ignore
A man till he won't stand it, for anything.
Put him to bed in the dark, at the top of the house,
And tell the lady in the black jet
He's a very difficult child. It's all black jet
As far as your mind can penetrate. I'm a man
Who will dare anything for a ha'penny night-light.

1ST GUARD. They've been looking for you, Captain Gettner.

GETTNER. What shall we say to them, Rusti? Whatever you suggest.

1ST GUARD. You're in serious trouble, sir. You've done it now.
You've made the mistake, God rest your soul.

GETTNER. You forestall me, you rascal Rusti.
If not, what do you mean by addressing the dead
With your hat on? I came to see my wife.

[62]

When there's trouble going on, and you know it,
And they won't let you out of the cage,
You fret until you don't know what you do.
You know family trouble, Rusti.

1ST GUARD.   Well, sir . . .

STEFAN. What's he doing?

GETTNER.   Three incorrigible;
  Three incorrigible traitors, can't help it:
  The heart, that's one, the brain, that's the second,
  And the will, old will power, deserters to the death.
  Shoot me now, and tomorrow you can join me.
  My wife has married another man.

STEFAN.   Heaven's name,
  You won't let him go on, Peter.

1ST GUARD.   Well, I see
  There's no pleasure in that, sir.

PETER.   The simple truth
  In a way, Stefan. If he can drink himself
  To safety, let him.

2ND GUARD [*to the* 1ST]. He's making trouble for us.
  If we keep with orders we know we're in the good.

GETTNER. Very sensible; keep to holy writ.
  The good sheep give no trouble going to market.
  I see your soul shining out in your buttons.
  You're a good, right-thinking soldier, Beppy.
  I must shake you by the hand, where is it?
  Let me shake you by the hand, virtuous fellow.
  You make sure I'm shot today, and join me
  When they command the last breath out of you.

2ND GUARD. I'll knock stars into anybody
  Who says I'm virtuous, and you can charge me.

GETTNER. Don't be sad, Beppy. No tears for me
And I promise there shall be no tears for you.
Don't let a difficult child who's lost his wife
Get in the way of promotion. And before
You die, Beppy, though I hope you live
To be very obedient for several weeks yet,
Say to yourself when you look at the stripe on your arm,
'Here's the last will and testament of Captain Gettner.'

2ND GUARD. I don't know why you have to choose
To walk into us, and in front of witnesses.

COUNTESS. None of us can be called a witness. There are times
When our very so-so vision can rescue itself
Only by failing altogether. I am sure
Neither of you wish to arrest him, and I
Have given my word to the Colonel that Captain Gettner
Shall not be allowed to cross his path. You had better
Undo your collars and sit down again.

1ST GUARD. But, ma'am—

COUNTESS. And I hope if Captain Gettner
Can't be persuaded to stay in hiding, he will help us
By being only apparently among us.
And I would say to him if he were here
That I have given my word to the Colonel also
There should be no offence to him tonight
If we all met together. And no offence—
This is my own promise to myself—
No offence to men who ask no questions
Of their endurance, but endure to live
As these men do. If he were here
I should beg him to remember that.

GETTNER. What did I tell you? Or if I didn't tell you
I tell you: Never come up to expectations,

[64]

They'll expect again, and quite differently.
They tell you to be a man of decision,
To take the cold sea in a courageous plunge,
And when you do they squint at you for a fool.
It's the ontological feminine principle.
God's a woman. That surprises you,
But it's perfectly evident in every aspect
Of the arrangement. Create you to think
You're the beloved of God, the blest
Pair of you in a confederation of longing,
With the whispers hot in your ear: Immortal man,
Immortal man achieve me.—And then
You're made another generation of:
The frank daylight's turned full on you,
And her finger withers you with scorn.

BELMANN. Gettner, go and tell your troubles to the Colonel,
Or, if you're staying, try and be tolerable.

GETTNER. I've no troubles; I mislead you.
I have a very interesting wife
Who, for the turn of a leaf, would love me.
Dear slug, she said, I'll be your faith. And so
She is, and here she is. Penelope's
Her name. I'll embrace her in open court
And you all can see the truth of it.

COUNTESS.   The truth
Will find its own time of authority, Richard.
It needs no demonstration.

PETER.   Gettner,
We can't make any accurate judgement of you
Until you're sober. But that's my last
Excuse for you. Move away from Gelda.

GETTNER [*to* GELDA]. Let me kiss you, or else they'll laugh at me.
[GELDA *makes no move*. GETTNER *kisses her*.

PETER. Extortion by pathos is a poor business,
　　Gettner. So it would be to use my hands
　　On a man who only half knows what he's doing.
　　But a man who mistakes his way can expect to be shown
　　The road. If you're not quiet now
　　I'll see you will be.

GETTNER.　　　　　You're very sure
　　Which is the mistaken man. Strange world,
　　If the worthy don't get all the prizes,
　　I agree, dear fellow; and I'm very sorry
　　You should ever taste failure, on my word
　　It's a shame; but Gelda remembers she once married me,
　　And has an idea to love me. That seems reason
　　Enough to kiss her in the sight of this congregation,
　　Without disrespect to anybody.

STEFAN. No, it's not true: you're lying!

GETTNER.　　　　　　　　Well, of course
　　That should really be the answer; Gettner's lying.
　　But then we have a beloved truth with us
　　Waiting to bear out what I say. Are you
　　Afraid to ask her, Zichy?

PETER.　　　　　I'm afraid to guess
　　How much deeper we shall have to sink
　　Before we find your lowest mark. But now,
　　For the time, we won't go lower than we are.
　　This can rest.

STEFAN.　　　Gelda, why don't you deny it?

PETER. I said it can rest. The man's in the mood
　　For a brawl in the street. But we won't
　　Give him satisfaction here.

[66]

GETTNER.   Satisfaction,
O God, satisfaction.

GELDA.   I think I told him so.

STEFAN. You think!

GELDA.   I told him so.

PETER. It could be. I can see it could be.

BELMANN. Man, you know him.
For goodness' sake, what do his tricks amount to?
He can't touch you.

PETER.   No, no, nothing
Essential.

JAKOB [*to* GETTNER]. Have you now made peace with yourself?

GETTNER. Can't keep things how they should be.
Well, I know I'm drunk.

COUNTESS. How shall we manage, with time at a standstill?
We can't go back to where nothing has been said;
And no heart is served, caught in a moment
Which has frozen. Since no words will set us free—
Not at least now, until we can persuade
Our thoughts to move—
Music would unground us best,
As a tide in the dark comes to boats at anchor
And they begin to dance. My father told me
How he went late one night, a night
Of some Hungarian anxiety,
To the Golden Bull at Buda, and there he found
The President of your House of Deputies
Alone and dancing in his shirtsleeves
To the music of the band, himself
Put far away, bewitched completely
By the dance's custom; and so it went on,

[67]

While my father drank and talked with friends,
Three or four hours without a pause:
This weighty man of seventy, whose whole
Recognition of the world about him
During those hours, was when occasionally
He turned his eyes to the gipsy leader
And the music changed, out of a comprehension
As wordless as the music.
It was dancing that came up out of the earth
To take the old man's part against anxiety.

1ST GUARD. That's so, ma'am; I've known my village
(Mindszent, I come from) on best occasions
Dance over the church clock striking
Till so dark you couldn't know
Where your feet would meet the ground
And not give over till the dusk of morning.

2ND GUARD. Rusti's the fellow to do it for you, ma'am.

1ST GUARD. What are you saying? I make a kick and go lifeless
If the music doesn't manage me.

> [2ND GUARD *plays a few notes on a mouth-organ.*

COUNTESS. Yes, you must give him the music; I'm sure it will
manage him.

1ST GUARD. Shall I, ma'am?

COUNTESS. Yes, indeed you shall. Clear a space for him!
Before long we shall all be dancing.

JAKOB. Dear Countess, not I!

BELMANN. Dance? I should never walk again.

> [*The* 2ND GUARD *begins to play. The* 1ST GUARD *takes off
> his belt and pistol-holster and lays it on the ground.*

1ST GUARD [*ready*]. If you want me to try, put it in funeral time.

[*The* 2ND GUARD *slows the rhythm a little. The* 1ST
GUARD *begins to dance. When the dance is well and truly
going the* 2ND GUARD *puts away the mouth-organ and gives
rhythmic shouts while he also takes off his belt and holster
and lays it beside the other, and his jacket also, and joins
the dance. The* COUNTESS *punctuates the dance with
rhythmic clapping, and* JAKOB *follows her.*

STEFAN *makes his way to the holsters, takes out the pistols
and puts them in his pockets while everyone's attention is on
the dance. He makes his way down to* GETTNER *and half
leads, half pushes him a little farther away from the others.*

STEFAN. You'd better come outside with me, Gettner.

GETTNER. What's the matter?

STEFAN.   Come outside; I'll tell you
What's the matter.

GETTNER.   It's cold outside.
You don't need to tell me anything.
Go to bed somewhere. I'm not interested.

STEFAN. Aren't you interested? Come out.

GETTNER.   You
Look after yourself. I'm a peaceable man.

[*Under cover of clapping from the* COUNTESS *and* JAKOB,
STEFAN *smacks his hand across* GETTNER'S *face.* GETTNER
sways on his feet. STEFAN, *when he has made sure that*
GETTNER *has lost his temper, backs slowly away, smiling,
to a doorway.*

GETTNER. You won't do that. No, no, no, by Christ Almighty.
[*He follows* STEFAN *out.*

The dance comes to an end.

[69]

COUNTESS. Good, good. You shall take breath.

[*The* 1ST GUARD *lies full length on the floor.*

JAKOB. What, are you going to ask them to dance again?
  Dear Countess, you and I will be dead with exhaustion.

COUNTESS. I want to learn the song they sing,
  The song I heard them singing on the march,
  The song that led you through the snow, Corporal,
  Lie where you are and sing it to me.

2ND GUARD. What song's that?

COUNTESS.   Why, a song. Yesterday
  You were very fond of it.

1ST GUARD [*singing from the floor*].
                  'For God and right we raise the cry
                  To crush our enemies or die,
                  And grind them with our heel.
                  With bloody sword we'll smite the foe
                  And rivers of their blood will flow,
                  And drench our valiant steel.'

COUNTESS.   No, no, Corporal.
  I learnt that as a child from my governess.
  It wasn't that.

2ND GUARD.   Do you think the lady means
  'Pretty Thomasina'?

                  [*The* 1ST GUARD *gives a whistle of dismay.*

COUNTESS.   Perhaps I do.
  I shall know when you sing it.

                  [*The* 1ST GUARD *sings a tune half-heartedly.*

  It is the one. But yesterday you sang it
  As though there were no other song in the world.
  What are the words of it?

1ST GUARD.   Ma'am, the words aren't special.

[70]

COUNTESS. Neither will my singing of them be.
Let me hear them.

1ST GUARD [*sings*]. 'Why so shy, my pretty Thomasina?
Thomasin, O Thomasin,
Once you were so promisin'.'

COUNTESS. Are these positively the words, Corporal?

2ND GUARD. You'd better be obliged for what he gives you,
ma'am.

COUNTESS. Very well, I will be. [*Sings.*] 'Why so shy', &c.
And then, Corporal?

1ST GUARD [*Sings*]. I shall woo you on my concertina.
[*Embarrassed.*] La la la la la la la—
[*Triumphantly.*] Thomasin-a!
[*The* COUNTESS *and the* GUARDS *sing the song again.*
Two pistol shots from outside. The GUARDS *make a rush*
for their holsters.

2ND GUARD. The Austrians, Rusti! They've surprised us!

1ST GUARD. A trap, they've set for us. Who's got our pistols?
Gone blinding into it. Oh, ma'am. What
Did we deserve this for?

2ND GUARD.   Who's got our pistols?

COUNTESS. Who has done this to them?

BELMANN.   Where is Gettner?

1ST GUARD. That Gettner! We had the chance of him
And let him twist us well and truly.
Now what do we say to them?

2ND GUARD. I said we should keep to orders.

PETER.   You have my word
There's no trap. I have an altogether
Different fear.

[71]

COUNTESS.   Where has Stefan gone?

> [GETTNER *appears in the doorway.*

GETTNER. Rosmarin, Rosmarin.

COUNTESS.   What are you saying to me?

GETTNER. It was nothing I did. I swear to you,
Rosmarin, I swear to you I aimed
Deliberately wide. I shot
Well wide of him. The boy
Was clear enough where he stood. Something
Turned the bullet. I didn't shoot him.

PETER. What does he mean for God's sake?

1ST GUARD. Stay still. We're here to see you stay.

BELMANN. Well, did you leave him there? Is that
The way to have left him? Wait, Countess, wait:
We'll go.

JAKOB.   We'll bring him here to you.

> [*Exeunt* BELMANN *and* JAKOB.

COUNTESS. Where is Stefan, Richard?

GETTNER.   Why me, why me?
I didn't make the gust of a wind, the tree-trunk,
Or whatever it was killed him. I aimed away.
I was laughing him off, but I heard him fire
And the bullet coming. I did refuse to meet him.
Before God, I said No, I said No, no, no.

COUNTESS. Richard, give me a quiet answer
To what I need to know from you.
You must say to me, Stefan is living.

GETTNER. He made me go with him, he made me mad.
But outside I was sober, outside the mist was clearing;
I aimed away, at a low star. But then

[72]

I felt him shoot, and my body jarred
From head to foot, and my pistol fired.

COUNTESS. Then say Stefan is dead. Say to me
I've killed Stefan.

GETTNER.   No!

COUNTESS.   Is Stefan dead?
All I am asking, Richard,
Is the courage of an answer. Not why;
But whether I go on without him.

Enter KASSEL.

KASSEL. I've come from Stefan, Rosmarin. Belmann
And Jakob tell me you've been given
A wickedly exaggerated account
Of what has happened.

COUNTESS.   Exaggerated?

KASSEL. Stefan is alive, Rosmarin.

COUNTESS. You've come to say so, little physician.
I hadn't let him go so easily.

KASSEL. The orderlies will bring him here. Rosmarin,
You must know he is hurt, but, the blessing of being so young,
New life will graft on a thread. By a stroke of luck
I was near when it happened. This precious idiot
Saw Stefan fall and went nowhere near him,
Belted off like a madman, and brought
His hideous farrago of nonsense to you.

1ST GUARD. It's come to this, the Captain's no use
To any of us. If we can get
Our pistols back, we'll take him to the Colonel.

[73]

2ND GUARD. Before he lands us in any more trouble.

BELMANN [*in the doorway*].
  I second your wisdom, Corporal. He's been
  Free too long.

1ST GUARD.   That's right.
  Back to plain duty. Send him to draw his pay.

COUNTESS. Corporal, have you children?

1ST GUARD.   Yes, ma'am, yes.

COUNTESS. Would you injure them, to please any opinion?

1ST GUARD. Ma'am, that's no question.

COUNTESS.   Then do not injure
  Mine. I mean my son. I ask you
  Not to make him the cause of punishment,
  Not to make his wound a death,
  Not to turn his challenge into a judgement.
  The stream of his life is running
  Shallow and slowly. Pray for him,
  Not because I love him, but because
  You are the life you pray for. And because
  Richard Gettner is the life you pray for.
  And because there is nothing on the earth
  Which doesn't happen in your own hearts.
  —Richard, let me have your arm to lean on.
  My body sometimes tells me
  I'm not here for ever.—Richard.

        RICHARD *makes no move. Enter* JAKOB.

JAKOB. Dear Countess, Stefan is coming. They're bringing him
  now.
        [*The* COUNTESS *almost falls.* KASSEL *and* JAKOB *support
        her. They try to lead her to a chair but she puts them aside.*

[74]

COUNTESS. No, no, that is over now. Perhaps for a moment
   He drew-in a draught of my strength. And now
   He comes on again with life, as I do. I can stand,
   I can welcome him. I need no help.

             THE CURTAIN FALLS

ACT THREE

The staircase, and the room, disfigured by the Hungarian occupation

[GELDA *is staring out of a window.* STEFAN, *in dressing-gown, moves into view upstairs, and* GELDA *hears him.*

GELDA. What is it, Stefan? What do you want? Get back to bed.

STEFAN. I know mother must be very ill.
I'm going to see her.

GELDA.   You're going to be well yourself
Before you start on any adventures.

STEFAN. She would have been to see me long before
If she hadn't been very ill.

GELDA.   Do you know
How narrowly and recently you've come
Back to us, Stefan? How carefully
You still have to obey us? Go back to bed;
Please, Stefan.

STEFAN.   She may be worrying about me;
But if she sees me there beside her
She'll know I'm all right again; we can improve
Together.

GELDA.   She will know you should never be there;
You will make it harder for her, not easier,
When she sees you looking more frail and paler
Than she ever dreamt you could. Keeping your bed
Is as much for her sake as for yours, Stefan.

STEFAN. When will she be well again?

GELDA.   When you are;
  Presently; together you can improve.

STEFAN. All right, but make sure of that. Tell her
  How nearly well I am.

                Enter BELLA.

BELLA.   Whatever is going on?
  Does the boy mean to give us more sorrow than ever?
  By making himself ill again? We pray
  God to keep him, and he makes it as difficult
  As can be. I suppose he means us all to go
  And cry round his bed when he's worse again.

GELDA. It's all been said, and he understands.
  He's going back to his room.

STEFAN [*as he goes*].   Good evening, Bella.

BELLA. He says good evening, as though I should answer
  Such wicked people.

GELDA.   Are you very good, Bella?
  How many days is it since you slept?
  My mother says make Bella sleep.

BELLA.   I rest
  Best when I'm watching over her.
  Once I begin to nod it all comes back—
  How they've broken this poor house to pieces
  And I think of it and I tell myself
  It's no good to worry, what can't be done
  Is beyond the angels; and that cause of it,
  That Gettner—

GELDA.   Richard Gettner has gone away.
  You needn't think of him now. Forget him, Bella.

BELLA. What has he ever done good enough to forget?

                    [77]

GELDA. The revolution's over,
    I'm sure it's over. The whole of yesterday
    We heard the guns, and today there's nothing
    But the noise of the rain. All night I was hearing
    The scattered solitary horsemen
    Galloping down the road; there was no
    Dead-march drum of the guns any longer.
    I heard the wind, and I heard the hail,
    And I heard the hoof-beats, and otherwise
    There was peace.

BELLA.   There's no
    Pleasure in fair weather when the stooks are black:
    Except that, now it's over, we shall see
    Count Peter coming to take you home.

GELDA.   I pray so.
    But if I should never see him again
    I've made myself into an enemy
    I shall never defeat. Bella, he went away
    Believing—

                            [*Hammering at the outside door.*

        I think he has come.

BELLA. That may be; you can't tell.

GELDA. Go to the door, Bella. No, no, I shall go.
                            [*She runs to the door and stops.*
    How do I know? It may be someone bringing
    News; almost any news.

BELLA.   Let me see
    What the truth of it is.

GELDA.   Well, hurry, then,
    And call out to me.

[78]

BELLA.   If it isn't the best news
  I open the door to, there's no hurry
  To call out any other.

                                    [*Exit* BELLA.

GELDA [*calling after her*].
  If you won't call out, perhaps I shall come with you,—
  I don't think I'm ready, I don't think so.

                            [*She goes to the window.*
                            The rain;
  I wish it would wash the last few days away.

                    Enter PETER.

  Peter! Now you're safely out of it all.

PETER. No one is safely out of it ever.
  It goes on, Gelda.

GELDA. I was telling myself it was over.

PETER. I have to go to Vienna.

GELDA.   Why, Peter?

PETER. You had to know where I was; that
  Was the only reason for coming here.
  But I should have been in Vienna long ago.

GELDA. Was that your only reason for coming?

PETER. The Hungarians are broken completely.

GELDA. It was what you were afraid of.

PETER.   I was afraid
  They'd lose the liberties they were beginning to gain
  Lately; not that we should lose the humanity
  We took of God two thousand years ago.

GELDA. Peter, what is it?

                    [79]

PETER. The government is shooting and hanging
  Every Hungarian of note who fought in the war.
  They're holding contemptuous, contemptible
  Courts-martial on the field, and executing
  Men, one after the other—men
  Whose families have given generations
  Of service to the Emperor.

GELDA.   On whose authority
  Can they dare to do this?

PETER.   Schwarzenberg's,
  In the name of the Emperor. What torments me
  Is whether I might not have prevented it
  If I'd never left Vienna: whether that ride here,
  Whether Stefan's message of alarm for Rosmarin,
  Wasn't one cause of these deaths and the endless consequences
  I'm too late, but I have to go there.
  And, though I'm too late, every moment here
  Makes me feel I'm betraying someone.

GELDA. You have to go; very soon.

PETER.   I have to go
  Forty-eight hours ago. You can give me
  Your prayers for what's already hopeless.
  I'll get word to you when I can.

GELDA.   Peter!
  Shall we say anything about ourselves?

PETER. There's going to be time for that.

GELDA. How do you know there's going to be time?
  I know I shall sit here, after you've gone,
  Making for myself a hundred accidents
  Which would mean I could never talk to you again.
  I can see the road to Vienna

A river of drifting, hopeless,
Dangerous men. And then I see myself
Telling myself for the rest of my life
What I should have said to you.

PETER.   You make me think
I shall betray something either way,
Staying or going. If I stay, I think
Of nothing but getting to Vienna. If I go,
I think of nothing but what you have said to me.
Say it to me.

GELDA.   Now I know it will take
A century to tell you. I could wish
You needed to listen as anxiously
As I need to explain to you.

PETER.   In the still of my mind
I do.

GELDA. In the still of my mind
I know I've never done anything to hurt us;
Only in the wandering, so easily cheatable
Part of me, where a right thought—
Or at least an excusable thought—suddenly
Finds it has taken pity on a horde
Of domineering wrong ones. It may have been right,
That first instinct, to put out with a lifeboat
For Richard, but on to it scrambled
Such a crew of pirates, my curiosity,
My pride, my ambition to succeed
Where I failed before, my longing to discover
What conversions could be made by love,
We all began to sink. And it was Stefan
Who rescued me, when he nearly died for the truth;
You and I are the truth.

PETER.   If that contents you
    It will always content me.

GELDA.   I don't know whether
    You're hurt or angry.

PETER.   Neither; I love you,
    But I'm impatient.

GELDA.   It would be a wry joke on me
    If it were you, not Richard, who turned out
    To be the intractable one I had to subdue.
    I thought I'd almost brought our world to an end,
    But you didn't greatly notice it.

PETER.   There have been
    Many things in my heart, and you and I
    Were not the least of them. But other worlds
    Come to an end tonight, Gelda,
    More irreparably than ours. That's why
    I have to go.

GELDA.   And, now I've said my say,
    I wish you were there already,
    I wish you had ridden straight there without thinking about me.
    It must be possible still to make Schwarzenberg
    See reason.

PETER.   A little late.

                Enter JAKOB *and* BELMANN.

BELMANN.   Why, Zichy,
    How do you manage to be here? Have the Hungarians
    Come to grief?

PETER.   To grief, certainly.
    So have we.

BELMANN.   In what way, so have we?

[82]

GELDA. Don't keep him now.

JAKOB.   Why off so soon?

PETER. We're celebrating victory
By executing every considerable officer
We can lay our hands on. I think someone
Should go and ask them why.

GELDA [*outside the door*].   Hurry, Peter!

PETER. And I'm going to ask them why.

[*Exit* PETER.

BELMANN. So he should. Though the degrees of distinction
Between admirable, permissible, and outrageous slaughter
Haven't yet been made perfectly clear to me.
I understand we should lament an earthquake
And prepare to contrive an earthquake
With equal zest.

JAKOB.   It's something to know
The revolution's over. After living
This marooned sort of life for so many days
We can welcome a return to normal.

BELMANN. With Gettner gone, the world does take on
A slightly more encouraging appearance.

Enter KASSEL, *by the lower door*.

JAKOB. Really, out walking, Dr. Kassel, in this terrible weather?

KASSEL. The ostler's wife came to the conclusion
The world could do with another young woman. Not
My place to contradict; though on the face of it
An umbrella would have been more sensible.
If circumstances hadn't seen
I was somewhere handy, old Doctor Brünn would have had
A hard, filthy ride here, through all manner of disaster,
And come into the bedroom (I've seen him do it)

[83]

Saying What's all this about, what's all this about?
As though he would deliver the child once
But that would have to be the end of it.

JAKOB. How are they now, the two of them?

KASSEL.   The mother's
Pleased with herself; the child can't disguise
An extreme disgust at the whole affair.
Well, they'll come to some working arrangement.—
So the revolution's come to a bad end, they tell me.

BELMANN. Zichy says the Government is making
Examples of them; brute vengeance going on.

KASSEL. Ah, is that so? They're determined the world shall have
Incident; they mean the historians
Never to fail for matter. Don't depress me
Any further.

JAKOB.   One always thinks if only
One particular unpleasantness
Could be cleared up, life would become as promising
As always it was promising to be.
But in fact we merely change anxieties.
In a day or two the road to Vienna
Should be clear to take again, but I hardly
Know what to do. No road is clear
Until the Countess is out of danger.

Re-enter GELDA.

KASSEL. There's no chance, I'm afraid, that Rosmarin
Will hold you here much longer.

JAKOB.   What are you saying?

BELMANN. Is it so serious? That's difficult to grasp.
You would think she would somehow have taken
The world with her.

JAKOB.   Do you really mean
   There's no hope, Kassel? No grain of hope?

KASSEL. We can count a day, perhaps: a day or two,
   But I can't promise more, even remembering
   How well her spirits will always argue
   Against the doubts of her body. After that
   The hours we have with her will be gifts
   Out of the air.

GELDA.   I think today she knows it,
   And seems willing. At least, suddenly
   She wrinkled her forehead, her eyes laughed,
   And she raised her hand in the way she does
   When she has been convinced by an argument
   She completely disapproves of.

BELMANN. Kassel, will you cast your eye? Upward.
   Is this in order?
                    [*The* COUNTESS *is descending the stairs.*

JAKOB.   Wonderful!
   It's our world revived.

KASSEL.   Our world a fool,
   I'm sorry to say.

GELDA.   Shall I go to her?

KASSEL. Wait a moment, wait a moment.
   Her body won't save her; there's no harm in seeing
   What comes of a still willing spirit.

BELMANN. She has a great ambition.

JAKOB.   A great spirit.

KASSEL [*calling to the* COUNTESS].
   Well, Rosmarin, so you've planned
   To take us by surprise.

[85]

COUNTESS. Now I know why a snail has eyes
    Which reach so far in front of him.
    He is too impatient to be there.

KASSEL. Would you take my arm, if I come to you?

COUNTESS.   No, no;
    If you will be patient I will be persistent.
    Within my experience there's never been
    Anything so precariously promising
    Since I first faltered
    Five steps into the lap of my grandmother.
    Which I can't remember. But great things came of it.

GELDA. Darling, wait to talk until you come to us.

COUNTESS. Ssh!

BELMANN.   I don't know when I hung on each moment
    In such fascination, unless when I watched
    A fishing boat outwit the rocks and a very
    Unbenevolent sea. It did at last
    Gain the shore.

GELDA.   Now, surely, for this last
    Easy level, which isn't worth defying,
    You can let me take you.

COUNTESS.   Well, I will,
    And then I can talk again.

JAKOB.   Dear Countess,
    How welcome you are you can never know.

COUNTESS. I welcome myself, too. It felt as though
    You had all fled to the Antipodes.

KASSEL. It's now my business to lecture you, seriously.
    While I do, you can be as inattentive

As you always are. But you pay me to give you advice.
And, in the name of my honest profession, I will.

COUNTESS. Little physician, I'll waive your fees
If you'll allow me my own legs,
At least when I need them.
I've been making, in retrospect, some calculations
By the sun, though the sun has been obscure,
And it seems to me today is Thursday!

JAKOB. It is, you know! We overlooked it
With all the anxiety, but today is Thursday!

COUNTESS. And when the last Thursday comes,
Which may be this one, I should like to be present.
So many years of meeting deserve to end
In a rare parting. It's quite true, the world
Being uncertain, I may spoil it all
By being here again next Thursday. But I'd rather
Go out, after the style of a night-light,
In a series of apologetic returns,
Than leave without ceremony, which would be surely
Ungracious to an earth which has entertained me.

KASSEL. Why not spare yourself, Rosmarin, for those returns?
Give to illness the same respectful hearing
I've seen you give to bores and fools.

COUNTESS.   Respectful?
I've been reverential. I've heard illness out
Until it has nothing more to say to me,
And I thank God I have the last word.

BELMANN.   But that
May be many years away.

COUNTESS.   You don't think so,
And I can't think of any praiseworthy reason

[87]

Why you should say so. Tell me instead
What is the news of the world I'm leaving?
Where is Richard Gettner?

GELDA.   Richard has left.

COUNTESS. Left for where?

GELDA.   He didn't say.
A horse has gone from the stables, and Richard
Has also gone.

COUNTESS.   Which horse?

GELDA.   Xenophon.

JAKOB. Don't be hurt again by that fellow.
Nothing he does is worth a thought.
Now he turns on his heel
After doing you such injury.
Afraid to look at what he's done,
And leaves not one word in compensation.

COUNTESS. I wish he hadn't taken Xenophon.
Xenophon's got a saddle gall.
I hope Richard will notice, and think of him.
But no cure comes by sighing, and I can't
Go off in pursuit, wherever they've gone.
Only, if any of you hear of Richard,
Ask after Xenophon.
We must value this evening as the one
Thursday in the universe, for the rest
Have gone, and no more may come,
And we should be on our most immortal behaviour.
I see that nothing of the sort can be expected.

BELMANN. If it entertains you, if you insist,
We'll make believe this is to be a farewell.

[88]

COUNTESS. You're very grudging.

JAKOB.   It's impossible!
   How can you bear to think of it?

COUNTESS. But you've always thought of it, Jakob,
   In the pleasure and conversation of these evenings.
   The argument, philosophy, wit, and eloquence
   Were all in the light of this end we come to.
   Without it there would have been very little
   To mention except the weather. Protect me
   From a body without death. Such indignity
   Would be outcast, like a rock in the sea.
   But with death, it can hold
   More than time gives it, or the earth shows it.
   I can bear to think of this:
   I can bear to be this, Jakob,
   So long as it bears me.   [*Someone taps on a window.*

JAKOB.   Who's that? What is it?

COUNTESS. Who can it be?

BELMANN. I see who it is, or who it has been.
   If the Hungarians have been smashed, then this
   Is an apparition off the battlefield.
   What do we do about him? Are you prepared
   To entertain another world?

COUNTESS.   But, of course,
   I'm ready for whoever cares to haunt me,
   Though I think a living man will haunt the world
   More desperately than anything out of the grave.
   Let him in.
            [*JAKOB opens the window.* COLONEL JANIK *enters.*

BELMANN. I'm not sure how to address you, Colonel. Are you
   Dead or alive?

[89]

COUNTESS.   Are you ill or distressed,
   Colonel? It's alarming to see you.
   What are your cares now? And why
   Do you come to my window?

                              [JANIK *cannot trust himself to speak.*
                       Is it more
   Harsh and necessary business
   Which if you could you would spare me? Colonel,
   First of all say any trivial thing;
   We shall come presently to the other.—Child,
   I know your cause is lost, but in the heart
   Of all right causes is a cause which cannot lose.—
   Your men, the men who stood here in the snow,
   They fought, Colonel, and they've been destroyed.
   Will you tell me?

JANIK.   They fought, and nothing's left.
   Who came out of that isn't worth saving.

COUNTESS. You mean yourself.

JANIK.   No, madam, I'm not out of it.
   None of us who had command
   Is to be left alive to think liberty.
   By now they know which way I slipped by them:
   It won't be long before they're round me in a ring.
   But I thought Count Zichy might be here, Countess.
   I thought he might let me have one word with him.

GELDA. He came not long ago and left again for Vienna.

JANIK. I came to tell him what Austria does to us.
   Excuse me; three times I've used your house
   Without civility. I won't again.

COUNTESS. Wait, Colonel. You're the man
   Who can help me to remember. There was a song

[90]

Your men sang while they were marching, they called it
Pretty Thomasina, and I began to learn
To sing the tune: all today
I've been trying to recall it.
Be so good, Colonel, remind me of it.

JANIK. Be so good, don't ask me for songs now.

COUNTESS. Be so good, you will remember it,
To save me teasing my memory any longer,
You will sing it.

> [JANIK *sings a few bars of the tune.*
> There it is; that's how it went.

—Colonel, it isn't safe for you to leave here.

BELMANN. Countess, it isn't safe for you to harbour him!

JAKOB. You've given yourself enough suffering already.

JANIK. I've not much wish for safety; and anyway
Nothing I can do is more than a postponement.

COUNTESS. No, no, you will stay here; that's decided.

JANIK. I neither want protection, nor would I ask
To be given it here. I've troubled this house enough.

COUNTESS. Then you won't want to put me to the trouble
Of persuading you, but simply hide yourself.

KASSEL. Rosmarin, nothing you've known will tell you
What you're asking to be faced with.

COUNTESS. They're men still who do this. I'm not faced yet
With hell itself. Away with you, Colonel.
You shall find the turret
By going left and right, and right and left again,
And there at an angle with the corridor

Is a door you will see, not much bigger than a child,
And through it a turning stair to the belfry.

JANIK [*going up the stairs*].
What am I letting you do? You'll find
These men are more determined. There's little chance
It will turn out well.

COUNTESS.   My wretched, failing memory!
Do, Colonel, put me in mind of the song again.
        [JANIK *sings from the stairs. The* COUNTESS *picks up the*
        song and JANIK *goes on and out of sight.*
There are better songs, of course.

BELMANN.   This is madness.

JAKOB. What do you mean to become of us all?

KASSEL. Rosmarin, I beg you, don't destroy yourself.

BELMANN. Haven't you any fear of consequences?

COUNTESS. There's one thing I'm afraid of.
I've become so absent-minded. My memory,
Desperate perhaps to forget nothing
Of my twenty-thousand days of life,
Is here, there, everywhere, but nowhere long,
Like a bat in a bedroom. So if I should confuse
My nationalities, or seem to be pleading
Richard's defence, instead of the Colonel's,
Do what you can to rescue me.
Say Pipistrello, and I'll draw back.

BELMANN. They may get quickly tired of the argument,
And decide that *we* have qualified for traitors
As well as Janik.

COUNTESS.   There is nothing
They may not do; there's no foolishness

They may not think; souls who will not budge
Out of their barren islands.

[*She begins to sing again.*

Enter RICHARD GETTNER.

GETTNER. They said you were dying.

JAKOB.   He can't come here!
What's to be done with him?

BELMANN.   With your permission,
Countess, we can quite easily
Persuade him to go.

KASSEL.   I definitely forbid
Any kind of disturbance.

COUNTESS.   Very welcome,
Richard. How is Xenophon?

GETTNER. They said you were dying, or dead. Otherwise
I should never have come from where I was,
Which was nowhere in particular, which suits me,
And nowhere long enough to stale the air
Too fatally. But how this rumour
Got where it did, is beyond all things
Extraordinary. Impossible anyone
Could have overtaken me and gone ahead.
I was going away from you at a full gallop.

COUNTESS. O Xenophon!

GETTNER. And yet every village had the story.
At the first inn I stopped at, the whole family
Came out to me, cousins and the lot,
Catching hold of the bridle and my boots,
Every face as wet as my shoulders.
Did I know you were dying? Was it true,

[93]

Were you dying? I told them
Not for another fifty years.
And when I couldn't convince them I pushed on.
But there wasn't to be any riding out of it;
The news had torn up your entire county.
Even the most outlandish hovels
Flung some creature practically under the horse
Shouting to know was it true you were dying.
If you weren't dying you were dead.
In the end I was so sick of the information,
And sick of seeing faces
Plastered with tears and rain, the road became
A nightmare and impassable.
So I turned round, which I now see
Was unnecessary. I should have stuck
To my first incredulity, and ridden
Straight on over the faces.

COUNTESS. And then I should never have known how well
They think of me; anyway how they care
About my leaving them. It makes me feel
Gross and unaccommodating
Not to bear out what they told you, Richard.
But it is a little irksome, always
To live up to the world's opinion in such matters.
I am proud of their tears. Now it will take
A life all over again to deserve them,
And I've hardly got to the end of this one.
Richard, forgive me, I've spoilt your journey,
And you've rewarded me with a great happiness.

GETTNER. Great hypocrite! You know I had no intention
Of giving you pleasure. And I wonder
You like to let your thirst for admiration
Lap up these tears.

COUNTESS.   As they were wept for me
   It's just as well I am here to appreciate them.

BELMANN. Will someone give me the word to get rid of this man?

JAKOB [*at the same time*].
   I can't and won't hold my tongue any longer—

KASSEL. No, no, no, for the sake of our dear friend,
   No quarrelling.

BELMANN.   Then perhaps Gettner
   Will show us how to admire him. There happens
   To be the opportunity, Gettner. Upstairs
   In the bell-turret, which you may remember,
   There's another fugitive hiding now:
   Colonel Janik. Convince the Countess, if you can,
   To keep this house innocent of any more disasters.

GETTNER. What claim has Janik on this house?
   What do you owe to Janik?

COUNTESS.   You need have no
   Concern, Richard. Colonel Janik hides here.

KASSEL. Rosmarin, unless you mean to distress me,
   Let me take you back to your room.

COUNTESS.   No, no:
   Richard has ridden a great distance to see me;
   But I see we're interrupting each other's pleasure.
   I suggest that for half an hour or so
   We should go about our devices. And my device
   Is to be left alone to talk with Richard.

KASSEL. But, Rosmarin, will you remember it's I who carry
   The responsibility?

COUNTESS.   I've always been willing
   As you know, to give you the credit for my health.

[95]

But you mustn't monopolize my death also;
That shall be quite my own. You shall come back
In half an hour, and find me
So well, I could go to bed. You must be
As trustful as I am when I take your medicines.
I prescribe you half an hour's absence.

KASSEL.   I take it
As you take my medicines, with appalling grimaces.

JAKOB. It goes very much against my heart
To leave you Countess; but since you wish it. . . .

BELMANN. Hardly a day passed in my boyhood
Without someone sending me out of the room.
I'm very well practised in withdrawing
As a matter of course, with the merest hint of surprise.

COUNTESS. It is so useful to have been a child.
Presently I shall long for you all to be with me.
                    [*Exeunt* KASSEL, JAKOB, *and* BELMANN.

GELDA. Richard, when you took Xenophon and rode away,
Neither you nor I, nor Peter, knew what following time
Was going to make of us. But you rode out
Of the indecision; and so did I. I think,
Mercifully, Peter and I have made our peace.

GETTNER. I'm not insensible of that mercy.

GELDA. I shall go up now and sit with Stefan.
Until the half-hour is over.

COUNTESS.   Tell him
I looked in and saw him for a moment
Splendidly sleeping.

GELDA.   He may be sleeping still.
                                        [*Exit* GELDA.

[96]

GETTNER. So it's true you're ill.

COUNTESS.   Oh, Richard, be careful.

GETTNER. What have I said?

COUNTESS.   For a moment I thought
You were trying to find words appropriate
To visiting the sick.

GETTNER.   Which you would find
Inappropriate and ridiculous.
But they'd be ten times less inappropriate
Than your detestable illness. And it is
Detestable, that you should be one more
Point of bleakness in a time
Already stark with punishment.
You can stoop your eyelids down, and make them
Close on a calm of mind.
But we don't live under your eyelids. There, perhaps,
By a serene elimination of
Three-quarters of the earth, you can exist
Beside the still waters. But out here
The drowning still goes on.

                    The COUNTESS *rests.*

                              And I'm the cause
Of this illness, I suppose.

COUNTESS.   The arithmetic
Of cause and effect I've never understood.
How many beans make five is an immense
Question, depending on how many
Preliminary beans preceded them.

GETTNER. But you haven't much doubt I brought this on you.
If I'm to be set loose, you shall be caught:

It's in the world's best manner.
The shrug of events, the *quid mihi est*,
So long as the punishment falls
It's inconsequential where.
And you let the cynical will be done, and I'm
To be saddled with the shame of it.
Rosmarin, you can consider this again,
And give up this threat of dying. I see there's to be
No living without you. I think you should marry me.

COUNTESS. I'm not going to ask you why. I shall quietly
Sit and let those astonishing words
Wash over me. They're contenting words
For any woman to have heard
As she goes where she goes. You, Richard!
You, of all men on the earth,
To be the one to say to dying things
'Be a beginning.'
And indeed, please God, to the last moment
I will begin; but not by marrying.

GETTNER. Why not? Why not by marrying?

COUNTESS.   It takes
Thought, and my thoughts are crowded. And some
Gravity, and I have an inconsolable
Inclination to laughter. And then, again,
Time: time to formulate,
Winnow, find, and have
A husband.

GETTNER.   Now so simple.
You love me, and I want to marry you.

COUNTESS. Tell me, Richard, what complication of logic
Made you think I loved you?

[98]

GETTNER.   There was never
  Anything better demonstrated.
  In the mythology of woman with man
  Show me a tale more certain, unswayable,
  Abundant, and long-suffering, than this
  Of you with me.
  Jealousy at the top of its fever
  Couldn't have found one hesitation
  To brood over and magnify.
  I acknowledge it.

COUNTESS.   Richard, Richard,
  What virtue I've missed! If only I'd thought
  Of being such a woman while there still
  Was time to try! What my memory
  Might not have done to future women in love
  To charge them with ardours of self-sacrifice,
  Half devotees, half nightingales, three-quarters
  Idiotic. I'm a fool to deny
  What you so beautifully praise me for,
  But truth leaps in me, and I have to confess
  I haven't loved you.

GETTNER.   You mean I haven't behaved
  In a way due to receive it.

COUNTESS.   I mean, simply,
  It never came about.
  There we have no free-will.
  At the one place of experience
  Where we're most at mercy, and where
  The decision will alter us to the end of our days,
  Our destination is fixed;
  We're elected into love.

[99]

So, Richard, whosever negligence it is,
I never loved you.

GETTNER.   I've nothing to say.
If you say so I can't contradict you.
I imagine it's more than ever satisfactory
To have done so much for a mere liking.

COUNTESS. Don't praise me; I never in my life
Was so unfit for praise. It would have been
Easier to love you than to like you, Richard.

GETTNER. I see you're determined to put me in my place.
You're going to insist on taking your revenge.

COUNTESS. If so, the revenge is on no one but me.
I'm not proud of being so insufficient
That I could like you no more than occasionally.
Just now I was very proud,
Thinking of all the villages in tears,
But I sit reproved,
A small, shameful bundle of prejudice.

GETTNER. You could like me no more than occasionally.
So that's it.

COUNTESS.   I'm not worth a thought,
I've put myself beneath your notice.

GETTNER. Will you tell me, then, what I meant to you?
A penance you gave yourself? Was I
An exercise in charity
Which is proving unfortunately fatal?
Isn't it a sort of insolence
To do for me what you care so little about?
What in God's name was it I meant to you?

COUNTESS. Simply what any life may mean.

[100]

GETTNER. I see myself reduced to one dimension;
  I'm not loved or liked by you. That fairly
  Disposes of me. I pity myself.

COUNTESS.   We need
  Neither of us despair. I'll not
  Leave you until I can love you, Richard.

GETTNER. It's no comfort to imagine us
  Clasped here indefinitely, anxiously waiting
  To love and be loved.

COUNTESS.   I don't mean
  Necessarily here.

GETTNER.   I'm not prepared to wait.
  I shall go back to the journey I was making
  In no direction in particular,
  Where the dark makes no false promises.
  I'll borrow, if I may, a fresher horse than Xenophon,
  And this time ride through the nightmare and not turn back.
  Your days are well rid of me, and so goodnight.

                                          [*Exit.*

              The COUNTESS *sings again.*

COUNTESS. There was more to come, so I imagine,
  But then they were interrupted.
  I wish I could go on singing.
  I am very much in love with something;
  What it may be I can't remember;
  It will come to me.
  That was a roundabout drive in the snow,
  Owing to my eccentric sense of direction!

                           [*A hammering on the door.*
                           [*Re-enter* GETTNER.

GETTNER. They're here, at the door, the Austrians for Janik,
  So you will understand if I avoid them

                        [101]

And go this way out to the stables.
You can't sleep now; you've given your word to receive them.
Rosmarin? Aren't you going to face them?
Do you mean this absolute no? Rosmarin.

> [*The hammering on the door.* GETTNER *goes to the window and opens it to make his escape. He turns to the* COUNTESS's *chair.*

You're dead, Rosmarin. Understand that.
What is there to stay for? You never showed
Any expectations of me when you were alive,
Why should you now?
This isn't how I meant that you should love me!

> [*He closes the window and comes back to her and speaks curtly.*

Very well, very well.   [*He stands beside her.*
> Be with me.
> > [*The hammering on the door.*

Enter BELLA.

BELLA. They must be quiet! How can I send them away
If they will come in?

GETTNER.   You can't send them away,
Bella, if they will come in.

BELLA.   But Madam—

GETTNER.   She knows
They're here. She says yes we're to let them in.
Go to the door, Bella, and let them in.

> [*The hammering at the door increases as* BELLA *goes out.*

THE CURTAIN FALLS

Melodies arranged and composed by
Leslie Bridgewater

HUNGARIAN DANCE

Mouth-organ

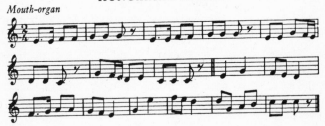

PRETTY THOMASINA

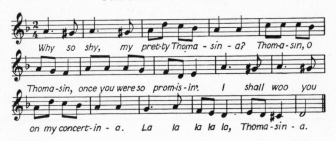

Why so shy, my pret-ty Thoma - sin - a? Thom-a-sin, O

Thoma-sin, once you were so prom-is-in'. I shall woo you

on my concert-in - a. La la ka ka la, Thoma-sin - a.

PATRIOTIC SONG

For God and right we raise our cry To crush our en - e

-mies or— die And grind them with our heel. With

blood-y sword we'll smite our foe And riv - ers of their

blood will flow— And drench our val - iant steel.—

[103]